SCHOOL COUNSELORS SHARE THEIR FAVORITE GROUP ACTIVITIES: A GUIDE TO CHOOSING, PLANNING, CONDUCTING, AND PROCESSING

Edited by:
Louisa L. Foss
Judy Green
Kelly Wolfe-Stiltner
Janice L. DeLucia-Waack

ASSOCIATION FOR SPECIALISTS IN GROUP WORK
Alexandria, VA

Published by
Association for Specialists in Group Work
5999 Stevenson Ave.
Alexandria, VA 22304

ISBN 978-1-55620-290-2

Table of Contents

Activities for Children

Activities for Adolescents and Pre-Adolescents

Activities for All Ages

Foreword
By Janice L. Delucia-Waack

Our first ASGW *Group Work Experts Share Their Favorite Activities* book was such a success, that we decided that the next step was creating one that was actually for those counselors who are the busiest and who probably lead the most groups: school counselors. So the idea of a *School Counselors Share their Favorite Activities* sequel was born. School counselors spend a significant amount of time leading psychoeducational and counseling groups and also facilitating classroom guidance activities, all interactions where structured activities are helpful and necessary. So our goal in putting together this book was to provide school counselors with a set of activities to be used to meet various goals that could be used with a range of age groups and in different settings in the school. School counselors and counselor educators from across the country were invited to share their favorite activities and to describe how to most effectively use them.

Each activity stands alone with a specific description of when and how to use it, goals, materials needed, directions, and how to process the activity to facilitate learning. We also included introductory chapters that we thought would be help to school counselors in developing a group program in their schools that was well-received by parents, administration, teachers, and students. The rationale and ethics of creating a vibrant group program in a school are addressed in chapters along with collaboration with other school personnel. How to effectively choose, implement, and process group activities are also addressed in other chapters.

Thank you to all who shared your favorite activities. We hope you enjoy this book and find the activities as useful as we did.

Chapter 1
Group Work in the Schools:
Moving Forward and Gaining Momentum
by Louisa L. Foss & Kelly Wolfe-Stiltner

One need not look far for a long list of concerns about the state of education, particularly in the United States. The myopic focus on federally-mandated assessment measures has led many educators to frustration and pessimism. Further, the current economic climate leaves schools with few, if any, resources to accomplish what is demanded of them (Smyth, 2008). Complicating these challenges is the wide variety of student issues, including increasing poverty, community violence, learning disorders, developmental disorders, and intolerance of social and cultural diversity, to name a few. It is in this atmosphere that school counselors must work, providing crucial social and emotional support for promoting academic achievement. Short on resources but long on demands, how can the school counselor best serve the intense, varied, and complicated needs presented by students?

Group Counseling: An Ideal Modality

For many student concerns, group counseling is an ideal modality for efficiently and effectively delivering counseling (ASCA, 1999; Riva & Haub, 2004). The American School Counselor Association (ASCA) stands behind school counseling as an important aspect of a comprehensive school counseling program (Lapan, Gysbers, & Petroski, 2001). Learning in groups and in relation to others is a common occurrence in the lives of children. For adolescents and pre-adolescents, peer groups become incrementally more important with each year and developmental stage. Skills in relating to peers and authority figures will be needed not only to succeed in the school environment, but in later adult situations as well.

Beyond social skills development, the group counseling context also provides a myriad of ways to grow intrapersonally. In a properly structured and intentional group counseling setting,

3

students can experience universality and decrease the social isolation that often accompanies emotional, behavioral, or academic problems. Common groups provided in the schools include those for academic skills, divorce, college/career preparation, self-esteem, anxiety, grief, anger management, and substance abuse (Steen, Bauman, & Smith, 2007). In this volume, a wide variety of topics are presented including worry (Amy Campbell's *Are You Growing Worries?*), school transition (Debbie Vernon's *Managing School Transitions*), self-esteem (Aaron Oberman's *Self-Esteem Sun-Beams*) and stress reduction (Rachel Vitale's *Breathe In, Breathe Out*). Other group activities in this volume aim to increase diversity awareness, develop academic skills, facilitate coping with military deployment, and improve anger management. These, like other groups, use the power of peers and social interaction to build a repertoire of new skills for use both in and outside of the group. Indeed, research supports the efficacy of group counseling for children in a variety of counseling settings (Hoag & Burlingame, 1997).

Group counseling is ideal for schools for practical reasons as well. With increasing case loads and demands on school counselors, group counseling allows school counselors to meet the needs of a number of children in a more efficient manner. In this way, group counseling can serve to benefit those participating and identify those who could benefit from more intensive school counseling or community mental health services.

Barriers to School Counseling Groups

Unfortunately, research suggests that a number of barriers stand between school counselors and the implementation of counseling groups. A study by Steen, Bauman, and Smith (2007) indicates that scheduling pressures and administrative duties make it difficult to conduct counseling groups. School counselors often carry a large student caseload or have administrative and other fair share duties that interfere with counseling duties. With the pressures of high-stakes testing, teachers and administrators are often hesitant to remove students from the classroom to work on what can be seen as non-academic issues. In many cases, it is critical to promote and 'sell' the idea of group counseling to school personnel and other stakeholders, so that adequate time and other resources can be committed to the planning and implementation of quality group counseling.

In spite of these challenges, it appears that school counselors continue to move forward with group counseling. Steen, et al (2007) found that of 802 members of ASCA surveyed, 87% conducted some form of group counseling in their schools. This number clearly demonstrates that in spite of the numerous challenges, group counseling is alive and well among ASCA members and that many school counselors recognize the promise in group work.

Solutions for Moving Forward

Implementing an effective school counseling group or group counseling program requires awareness of the issues relevant to students, school personnel, and families. The thinly-stretched resources of the school counselor will be best used if focused on the most critical and pressing student problems. DeLucia-Waack (2006) emphasizes the need for a needs assessment survey early in the process. An assessment may provide a list of potential topics for students to choose, and an indication of students' ideas regarding the potential utility of groups. The assessment data may then be used to assist in development of group goals (DeLucia-Waack, 2006). Concise, clear, and mutually-agreed upon goals can then be used to drive the group forward.

Another benefit of the needs assessment process is the opportunity to collaborate with school personnel. When teachers and administrators are included in the needs assessment process it helps them to understand how removing students from class can be beneficial to them by improving the classroom and school climate by addressing areas of concern in the school. Also, utilizing a group approach allows school counselors to reach more students in a more efficient manner and provides the benefits of normalizing student issues and learning from one another.

In addition, school counselors can also utilize groups to address national and state standards. With the current educational climate, schools are required to show how they are addressing standards and making progress towards them. School counselors can utilize groups to meet the standards set while providing easily collected data through pre and posttests during the group process to show they are making an impact. This also helps provide rationale for removing students from the classroom to participate in a group.

If most school counselors have an appreciation for the efficacy of group counseling in the schools, how can we promote the use of this modality to its fullest potential? How can school counseling groups address the social and emotional problems children experience that impair their academic performance? In essence, how can we continue to press forward as group counselors? As we often say to students, knowledge is power. Though research in school-based group treatments is sparse, increasing attention is being directed toward these interventions (Riva & Haub, 2004; Dagley, et al., 1994). School counselors can seek and share theoretical and empirically-based literature to both improve their own delivery of group counseling and defend the use of the modality to other stakeholders.

Though time is scarce, school counselors can use their own professional networks to provide and receive consultation so they feel supported in their practice as groupworkers. Through sharing ideas and energy for the group process, school counselors can encourage each other to overcome the barriers. Indeed, reminding each other of the beauty and potential in group processes among children can be a true motivator for giving the extra effort it requires to plan and implement a successful school counseling group. Though the challenges in school counseling groups are many, professional networks and resources can provide the momentum to overcome.

References

American School Counselor Association. (2005). *Position statement: The professional school counselor and group counseling.* Retrieved April 19, 2008, from http://www.schoolcounselor.org/content.asp?contentid=210

Dagley, J. C., Gazda, G. M., Eppinger, S. J., & Stewart, E. A. (1994). Group psychotherapy research with children, preadolescents, and adolescents. In A. Fuhriman & G. M. Burlingame (Eds.), *Handbook of group psychotherapy* (pp. 340-370). New York: Wiley.

DeLucia Waack, J. L. (2006). *Leading psychoeducational groups for children and adolescents.* Thousand Oaks, IL: Sage.

Hoag, M. J., & Burlingame, G. M. (1997). Evaluating the effectiveness of child and adolescent group treatment: A meta-analysis review. *Journal of Clinical Child Psychology, 26,* 234-246.

Lapan, R. T., Gysbers, N. C., & Petroski, G. F. (2001). Helping seventh graders be safe and successful: A statewide study of the impact of comprehensive guidance and counseling programs. *Journal of Counseling and Development, 79,* 320-330.

Riva, M. T., & Haub, A. L. (2004). Group counseling in the schools. In J. DeLucia-Waack, D. A. Gerrity, C. R. Kalodner, & M. T. Riva (Eds.), *Handbook of Group Counseling and Psychotherapy* (pp. 309-321). Thousand Oaks, CA: Sage.

Smyth, T. S. (2008). Who is No Child Left Behind leaving behind? *The Clearing House, 81,* 3, 133-137.

Steen, S., Bauman, S., & Smith, J. (2007). Professional school counselors and the practice of group work. *Professional School Counseling, 11,* 72-80.

Chapter 2
Matching Activities to Group Stage and Goals
By Janice DeLucia-Waack

Activities are an essential part of groups in the schools. Group leaders tailor activities to the main task inherent in the current group stage and overall group goals. From the very beginning of the first group session, all group activities, processing of group activities, and group discussions should emphasize group goals and norms such as self-disclosure, self-exploration, and feedback as they relate to the facilitation of group goals. There are several ways to think about using activities within the context of group work. Based on the type of group, individual and group goals, structure and format, the use of activities within the group will vary significantly. This chapter will review common mistakes in using activities and then guidelines are suggested for choosing activities based on the type of group, structure, group goals, and goals of each group session. Meaning Attribution is a key component in the effectiveness of activities; group members must be able to understand why they participated in an activity, what they did, and what they learned from it.

Common Mistakes in Using Activities

One of the most common mistakes in selecting an activity is because it is fun or because group members would like it. All group activities should have a focus on teaching skills related to communication, conflict resolution, and problem solving. Also important to remember is that group leaders must keep members on task to provide structure and safety, and effectively utilize time. Thus, a group leader in effect wastes time and diverts attention from the group goals and tasks by introducing an activity that does not clearly relate to group tasks at hand. Having said that, there are two issues to consider. One, sometimes groups do need to connect and laugh and share some common experiences without a lot of emotion or seriousness. Two, just about any activity can be useful if it is processed in such a way that facilitates the group tasks at hand. A later chapter will provide guidelines for how to effective process activities and suggest several frameworks for generating processing questions. J. Scott Glass's *Group Juggling* activity is a good example of an activity that encourages levity, humor, and laughter within group work, as well as asking group members to think about how groups work effectively in a non-threatening way. Group members are asked to juggle as a group, given an object (or objects) to pass throughout the group with directions of how to transmit the information about what the object is. Hutchins suggested different processing questions that included such questions as: how did we as a group work together during this challenge? How well is our group able to listen to one another and share ideas? What have we learned about working with others that will help us in future situations? Jeri Crowell's *Out with the Trash!* Is another activity that using humor to help group members vent about issues/problems in their lives.

There are several common mistakes related to how activities are conducted. Directions need to be very clear, specific to the age group, and sequenced appropriately. It is helpful to write the directions down ahead of time and to make sure that all words will be understood by the group members. Evaluation of the order and sequencing of the directions is also helpful. For older group members, you may be able to give them three directions at once. For elementary school students, you might give one direction, let them do that activity, give them another direction, etc. (draw a circle of the paper, wait, draw a symbol that represent you in the middle of the circle).

Underestimation and overestimation of time are two other common mistakes. Even with practice of specific activities, the amount of time needed to complete a particular activity varies significantly depending on the group. My solution to overestimation is to be over prepared and always have another activity with the same goals and topic ready if there is more time available. I also usually plan four to five processing questions for each activity, with the understanding that most likely I will choose the two or three that are most well relevant based on what happens in this activity for that particular group. If an activity takes less time than I anticipated, the group may discuss all of the processing activities related to that activity.

My solution to the problem of underestimation of time for a specific intervention is less than ideal. It is helpful to consider when planning an activity if there are any steps that can be omitted, that members can be asked to think about over the week, and then discuss in the next group session. Again, to save time the focus of Processing may only be on the one or two questions most useful as opposed to the three to five prepared.

There may be some temptation, and some pressure, to conduct the group around a table. In schools, groups are often conducted in classrooms or in the lunchroom. If at all possible, use a circle of chairs or sit on the floor in a circle, again emphasizing that this is a different atmosphere with different guidelines than other situations within the school. Others (Carrell, 2000; Smead, 2003) suggest using a table for creative endeavors but moving back to the circle to discuss and process. The table sometimes serves as a barrier to effective communication.

If at all possible, practice the activity ahead of time. Even if you participate as both group leader and member, you will have the experience of saying the directions out loud, gaining an estimate of how long an action takes, and recognizing potential problems.

Be prepared that the activity may not go as planned. Always consider the use of one or two processing questions that are directed at understanding why the activity did not work. For example, the group leader might ask: "the goal of this activity was to help group members to identify strengths that they could use to help other group members in this group. But most of you had a very hard time saying that you did anything well. What happened? What was it like to think about things that you did well? Could you think of any? If you could, what made it difficult to share with the group? What things inside of you made it difficult to share it with this group? What things that have happened in this group made it difficult to share with the group?

One of the most common mistakes group leaders make is not to process an activity. Indeed, most books on group exercises and activities do not include the direction or guidance that is necessary for effectively processing of activities (Kees & Jacobs, 1990). This is ironic since processing has been described as the most important phase in using group exercises. Yalom (1995) further emphasized that the experiencing of events in group is not sufficient for the facilitation of change. Rather, an in-depth process examination of the experience is necessary to be able to retain, integrate and generalize these experiences. Processing helps group members to understand what they have done, how they have contributed to effective group process, what new skills and behaviors they have learned, and how they can apply what they have learned to their outside lives. A later chapter will discuss guidelines and models for effectively processing activities.

Choosing Activities

Session Structure. Structure is essential to providing safety and continuity to the children. Structure is also necessary to manage time efficiently, and focus on relevant issues (DeLucia-Waack, 2006). Depending on the type of group and the age of group members, the level of structure may vary. The younger the group members, the more structure is necessary. Psychoeducational groups tend to be more structured with activities designed to facilitate discussion of a topic and/or development of new skills and behaviors. To make the transition from one group session to the next, it is helpful and creates a sense of trust to have a structure for each group session that is expected and predictable.

Group sessions typically include four parts. An Opening reviews material from a previous session, discusses homework efforts, and/or introduces the topic for this session. The Working part uses activities that focus on the goals of the group allowing discussion and interaction around a specific topic or skill to identify, learn, and/or practice potentially effective behaviors. Processing Activities typically include questions to help make sense of the Working activities and apply them to life outside of group. Closing Activities help group members to prepare to leave group.

Matching Sessions to Group Goals. It is important to decide prior to the onset of a group the sequence and contents of each group session because so much of what happens in group is interconnected. For instance in screening interviews, preparation sessions, and the first session, it is useful to describe group goals, typical group topics and themes, and interventions that will be used. Thus, those decisions need to be made ahead of time. In addition, any homework assigned during a session should lead logically into the topic and interventions that will occur in the following sessions. Moreover, it is important for group leaders to plan for the sessions in advance and gather group materials.

A general guideline for planning the group should be at least one session each for both opening and termination sessions, and one to two sessions focused on each goal. Generally, an 8 week psychoeducational group should have two to three goals. It would then be possible to spend five to six weeks on the content to meet these two to three goals.

Matching Interventions and Activities to Session Topics. Once group leaders have identified goals for a specific group, it is important to survey the literature to see what interventions are suggested to meet these goals and also what specific group sessions have already been designed to incorporate these interventions to achieve these goals. It does not make sense to reinvent the wheel every time a group leader leads a new group. This is probably one of the biggest deterrents to leading groups, particularly psychoeducational groups. Psychoeducational groups, as it has probably become evident by now, take a great deal of time to plan and to examine the literature, a luxury most group leaders do not have. This book is designed to help school counselors to use activities effectively and to find activities for their groups with minimal effort. Another book also published by ASGW, *Group Workers Share Their Favorite Activities: A Guide to Choosing, Planning, Conducting, and Processing* (DeLucia-Waack, Bridbord, Kleiner, & Nitza, 2006) also has 50+ activities categorized by stage of group with specific directions for all ages.

Matching Interventions and Sessions to Group Stages. One of the initial tasks inherent in group work is to choose an activity that is appropriate for the stage of the group you are working with. According to Yalom (1995), structured activities, when appropriately chosen, can serve to accelerate the group past a particularly slow or stuck phase of the group. Following the framework postulated by Jones and Robinson (2000), activities should be chosen based on the following three stages: initial, working, and ending. Group leaders should tailor activities to the main task or issue inherent in the stage that the group is currently working through. They also suggest that intensity should be a key determinant in the choice of an activity by stage. They define intensity as "the extent to which the group topic, structured exercises, and group techniques do the following: (a) evoke anxiety among the group participants, (b) challenge group participants to self-disclose, (c) increase awareness,

(d) focus on feelings, (e) concentrate on the here and now, and (f) focus on threatening issues" (p.358).

Initial stage activities should focus on building trust and introducing members to the group and to each other. Working stage activities should focus on assisting members to self-disclose, to become involved in the process of group, and to learn new behavioral and thought patterns to meet group goals. Ending activities focus on assisting the members in termination and bringing what they have learned to use once the group has ended. Thus, the chosen activity should focus on overcoming obstacles that are inherent in each respective stage.

Initial Stage. Activities used during the initial stage of the group should focus on helping the members introduce themselves to the group, meet their fellow members, and overcome their anxiety (Jones & Robinson, 2000). This stage is characterized by encouraging interactions that are of low intensity and focus on orienting members to the norms, processes, and interactions of the group. These activities should involve minimal affective components and should be non-threatening. The focus should be on decreasing, rather than increasing, the members' anxiety. As members tend to feel anxious and relatively unwilling to disclose, activities should parallel this constraint on interaction. Choosing an activity that focuses on high levels of disclosure and affect would be too intense and threatening for members at this stage. Typical activities focus on introductions, trust-building, and modeling appropriate behavior. Examples of activities for the initial stage include *Group Juggling* by J. Scott Glass, *My Roadmap* by Kara Ieva and Jacqueline Swank, and *The Computer Game* by George Leddick.

Middle Stage. The middle stage of group is characterized by intense affect, increased self-disclosure, and an accelerated willingness to work on one's own issues. As the group moves past the initial conflicts of safety and trust, a higher sense of cohesion develops, allowing for increased self-exploration and expression. Thus, members are more willing to take risks with the activities presented. Subsequently, activities chosen for this stage of group should be of high intensity. That is, these activities should encourage members to increase their self-awareness; increase affective involvement; take risks and try out new behaviors, skills, and attitudes; and work through personal issues that may interfere with trying out new behaviors and skill sets.

Activities for the middle stage of group should be challenging for the members as well as anxiety provoking. Through this, members will be assisted in contributing the appropriate amount of disclosure within the group. More intense activities will match the group members' increased willingness and eagerness to explore new ways of thinking and behaving. Activities at this stage might also assist members in working with conflict, recognizing a wider range of emotions and expressions, and focusing on the here-and-now. Activities that can be used during the working stage of group include Michael Lamke and Paula McWhirter's *Holding Hands: Teaching Children How to Find Support* which uses a DVD to teach children of divorce how to talk about their feelings and also normalize some of their reactions to the divorce or separation. Zulema Suarez and Hugh Crethar suggest an activity, *People First*, which helps children and adolescents to focus on who people are, not just their disabilities. Monica Hunter and Shannell Petty's activity, *Band-Aid Flipbook*, teaches decision-making within the context of how to deal with peer pressure. To help identify career aspirations, Angela Coker suggests an activity, *Thinking about Self and Career Development*, to encourage self reflection and then links it to interests and aspirations. David Hermon and Terri McConda's *Good Credit, Bad Debt* is a useful addition to a life skills group focusing on understanding about credit and making choices about debt.

Ending Stage. Activities that are chosen for the ending stage of group should focus on issues surrounding termination. In light of impending termination, members should move away from the high-intensity encounters and focus on the integration and application of new skills and attitudes. Thus, activities selected for this stage should focus on exploring what the members have gained from the group and how it will impact their lives in the future. Activities could also focus on helping the members say goodbye to each other and expressing what they have learned and gained from each other. Activities should be less intense than in the working stage, and should focus on assisting members achieve closure from the group. Examples of activities that are appropriate for the termination stage

15

of group include *Self-Esteem Sun Beams* by Aaron Oberman and *Look at Me in a Sugar Cookie* by Stephanie Markey.

Uses of Activities Related to Group Tasks

While many activities can be used to develop several therapeutic factors and address different group goals and tasks, it is how group leaders process the activity that determines the focus, direction, and application of learning for the group members. The section that follows will discuss different uses of activities in groups, suggestions on how to process these activities, and also provide examples of specific activities that could be used in psychoeducational groups for children and adolescents.

To Introduce Group Members To Each Other. In the initial stage, one of the primary tasks is to introduce group members to each other, focusing both uniqueness and strengths of group members, as well as connections and similarities between group members. Anxiety is high given the newness of the experience and the apprehension of sharing in a group of strangers. Activities used at this point should help members to self-disclose safely and then ask members to discuss what it is like to share, how they chose to take risks in group, and how they will continue to do this throughout the group.

Examples of activities that might be useful in this stage include Lenoir Gillam's *Completing the Puzzle* which asks group members to talk about their individual goals for group and also helps identify assets each group member will contribute to group. Processing questions focus on what they learned about each other, possible connections, and what they have learned about how to interact with each other.

In groups where children and adolescents may already know each other, it is important to use activities that will help group members get to know a side of each other that they would have not known from previous interactions. Rachel Vitale's *Building Bridges* asks group members to build a bridge without communicating to facilitate cohesion.

The Illumination of Group Process. The activities suggested in the above section are designed to help members get to know each other and will also reduce their anxiety as they start to make connections and feel more comfortable. Other activities that specifically helped to define the group process and make a concrete for group members are also helpful to reduce anxiety.

Examples of such activities include George Leddick's *Who's the Leader* which encourages members to focus on group process who playing a game. Other activities ask members to focus on their relationships with others in the group and how group members can work as a team, such as *From Here to There* by Imelda Lowe and Virginia Allen. Nikki Currie's *Circle of Hands* helps identify positive group norms.

To Teach And Practice New Skills. Activities designed to teach and practice new skills often include an instructional component along with a practice component. Sometimes it is useful to have students discuss and write down what their strengths are already in this area, potential strategies, and new skills; then lead into experiential activities such as role-plays and drama to practice the new skills. Even children and adolescents may already have skills in the area of communication, conflict-resolution, and assertiveness; yet they may not choose to use them. When group members possess essential skills and actively choose not to display them, one of the goals of the intervening is to help group members examine why they would choose not to use effective behaviors. Irrational beliefs, family concerns, and peer issues may all influence group members attitudes and behaviors.

Activities specifically designed to promote creative thinking, problem-solving, and brainstorming may be useful as introductory activities to create a framework of effective problem-solving that facilitates accomplishment of the group goal. Marie Horton, Amber Lange, and Amy Brown suggest an activity, *RAP (Repeat and Practice) Up Social Skills* that teaches self-control and cooperation while playing a game. Melissa Luke's *Feeling 4-Square* teaches how to identify and express feelings. *Coping Skills Links* by Jacqueline Swank and Kara Ieva teaches group members to distinguish between healthy and unhealthy coping skills and to create a list of healthy coping skills. Louisa Foss and Maria Foss Rand's *Personal Boundaries: Doors to My Heart* introduces the topic of interpersonal boundaries and teaches strategies to feel comfortable with their boundaries.

Some activities in this book teach very specific skills. *Breathe In, Breathe Out* by Rachel Vitale teaches the relaxing effects of deep breathing. *Memory Quilt* by Deborah Beck Smith and *A Collage of Memories* by Judy Green help group members in the grieving process. Kelly Duncan and Holly Nikels' *Staying Safe Online* first identifies potentially dangerous situations online and then brainstorms ways to keep group members safe and get help from an adult if something odd occurs. Melanie Korth and Pit Kolodinsky's *Handling Feelings about Deployment* helps group members share feelings about their family members' deployment and also teach coping skills.

To Provide Members With Feedback. Activities that focus on feedback have several different foci. The first is very specific, asking group members to comment on a very specific interaction, whether role-plays or an activity, with feedback given to all group members. Sometimes feedback is given to members based on perceptions over a series of group sessions and is focused less concretely on specific situations. It is also useful at various points in the group to reflect on how the group works together as a whole and to give the group as a whole feedback on what things to continue to do to make the group effective, and also what things might need to be changed to make the group more effective. Monica Hunter, Joel Lewis, and Andre Green suggest an activity, *I am Special*, that helps group members to identify positive aspects of themselves while also asking them to examine how to address negative feedback from others. The Hot Seat by Matthew Day teaches communication and conflict resolution skills by asking group members to give each other positive and negative feedback in a constructive way.

To Increase Self-Awareness. Useful activities to increase self-awareness include Stephen Kennedy and Holly Kayler's *Feelings of Anger* that helps identify when they are angry and ways to express the anger. Amy Campbell's *Are You Growing Worries?* provides a structure for group members to identify when they worry and to develop coping strategies when worrying is not productive. Colors of Memories (Negative) and Colors of Memories (Positive) by Bengu Erguner-Tekinalp helps children and adolescents share memories and examine how they influence the present. Nikki Currie's *For Girls Only* creates a concrete representation of each girl's positive characteristics using the letters of their name to create the symbol.

To Facilitate Closure and Consolidation Of Learning. As members contemplate leaving the group, examples of process comments relate to how their leaving might reflect familiar patterns of leaving and loss or how they will apply the insights they have learned in the group to both how they choose to leave and their lives outside of the group. Group members might write letters to themselves detailing what they have learned from the group and how they will continue to use their new skills that can be mailed to them. Group members may also go back to their goals that they verbalized or wrote down in the beginning of the group and evaluate their progress. The *Termination Capsule* by Melissa Luke creates a time capsule that reminds group members of what they have learned from group. The *Rainbow Web* by MaryLou Ramsey also helps group members to reflect upon and give feedback to group members about how group has been helpful to them.

Cautions

Even in psychoeducational groups, activities can be overused. Leaders may become overly dependent on activities using then in rapid fire succession, rather than recognizing the value in properly processing an activity. Allowing sufficient time for one activity and the careful processing of that activity to promote interpersonal learning, self-understanding, and practice of new skills and behaviors may be much more effective than quick completion of four activities on the same topic.

Creative arts activities, particularly those that involve drawing and cutting and pasting for collages, are very time intensive. Group time is valuable and so if time intensive projects can be assigned as homework, so much the better (e.g., hand out paper bags and magazines and ask members to represent themselves on the inside and outside of the bag to share in the next group session). Work outside of group reminds group members of what has happened in previous sessions and also helps them to prepare for future sessions. (Yalom used to send process notes to his group members strategically in the middle between group sessions to make them think of group between sessions.)

Activities and exercises may appear gimmicky (Gladding, 2000) to group members if they are overused and if they are not properly processed. Children and adolescents begin to see group as the place that they go to make things, not the place that they go to learn about themselves and make changes. Again, Meaning Attribution for all activities is essential. Also because the activities are used in groups, the goals should include in this order: learning about oneself, learning about how one relates to others, and learning about oneself as perceived by others. Thus, processing of activities should focus on the multiple levels of learning and activities. The earlier section that describes modeling of processing addresses this issue and makes sections on how to select processing questions that focus on the group members, interactions between group members, and the group as a whole.

It is also important in leading psychoeducational groups for children and adolescents that there be a balance of information delivery, skill development, and group processes (Conyne, 2003). Ideally, as part of the Working part of a group session, there should be a brief provision of information, sometimes a refresher of information previously discusses or sometimes provision of new information (3 to 5 minutes), some activity focused on practicing the skills, and then some time spent on processing the activity directed at identification of what group members have learned and how they will apply it.

References
Carrell, S. (2000). *Group exercises for adolescents: A manual for therapists* (2nd ed.) Thousand Oaks, CA: Sage.

Conyne, R. K. (2003). Best practice in leading prevention groups. *Group Work Practice Ideas: Association for Specialists in Group Work, 32*, 9-12.

DeLucia-Waack, J. L. (2006). *Leading psychoeducational groups for children and adolescents.* Thousand Oaks, CA: Sage Publications.

DeLucia-Waack, J. L. (1997). Measuring the effectiveness of group work: A review and analysis of process and outcome measures. *Journal for Specialists in Group Work, 22*, 277-293.

DeLucia-Waack, J. L., Bridbord, K. H., Kleiner, J. S., & Nitza, A. (Eds.) (2006). *Group work experts share their favorite activities: A guide to choosing, planning, conducting, and processing (Rev.).* Alexandria, VA: Association for Specialists in Group Work.

Dossick, J., & Shea, E. (1990). *Creative therapy II: 52 more exercises for groups.* Sarasota, FL: Professional Resource Exchange, Inc.

Gladding, S. T. (2000, Fall). The use of creative arts in groups. *Association for Specialists in Group Work Group Worker, 28*, 7-9.

Jones, K. D., & Robinson, E. H. III. (2000). Psychoeducational groups: A model for choosing topics and exercises appropriate to group stage. *Journal for Specialists in Group Work, 25*, 343-355.

Kees, N. L., & Jacobs, E. (1990). Conducting more effective groups: How to select and process group exercises. *Journal for Specialists in Group Work, 15*, 21-29.

Smead, R. (2003). Enhancing groups with youth through the use of props. *Association for Specialists in Group Work, Group Worker, 31*, 11-14.

Yalom, I. D. (1995). *The theory and practice of group psychotherapy* (4th ed.). New York: Basic Books, Inc.

Chapter 3

Processing Activities to Facilitate the Transfer of Learning Outside of Group

Karen H. Bridbord & Amy Nitza

What exactly is processing? According to Stockton, Morran, and Nitza (2000), processing can be described as "capitalizing on significant happenings in the here-and-now interactions of the group to help members reflect on the meaning of their experience; better understand their own thoughts, feelings and actions; and generalize what is learned to their life outside of the group" (p. 345). Lieberman, Yalom, and Miles (1973), in their description of the four types of effective leadership behavior, emphasize the importance of meaning attribution for group members in helping them to make sense of group events and then subsequently to apply what they have learned to their lives outside of the group. Jacobs, Harvill, and Masson (1988) described processing as the most important phase in using group exercises.

Processing is important because it allows participants to create meaning through reflection, sharing, connecting, and extrapolating. It is a creative endeavor that utilizes all of the participants' experiences. Philosophically, process is a means of translating the concrete to the abstract and it is an invitation to participants to co-create meaning and to be active in their own process of growth. Effective group leaders listen for themes (including those that come in metaphors) that are interpersonal, intrapersonal, and group-as-a-whole. A group leader who processes is much like a conductor of a symphony. Each member plays his/her own instrument and it is up to the conductor to listen to make sure that each musician is on key, to notice when they are not, and to help the orchestra function as a whole for the benefit of each individual musician, as well as for the benefit of the composition.

For students in schools, processing is a crucial aspect of group counseling in that it allows them to make meaning of their group experience and then apply that learning in order to be more successful in school. Doing so will not only be of benefit to students themselves, but as students display new behaviors, teachers and administrators will be able to observe the benefits of groups in their schools.

Why Process An Activity?

Processing questions are intended to help members reflect on their reactions to the activity, learn about themselves and transfer their learning to their real lives. Processing can be directed at various levels of learning: interpersonal, intrapersonal and group-as-a-whole.

Intrapersonally based questions are intended to help members gain personal insight. Examples of questions include:
- What have you learned about yourself?
- Were you surprised by your reaction the activity?
- How did you feel disclosing this information about yourself?
- How does that relate to your life outside of the group?

Processing questions that are interpersonally targeted allow members to learn about their interactions with others such as:
- What did you learn about others?
- How will this learning affect your interactions with group members?
- What similarities did you notice between your responses and others' in the group? Differences?
- Did you have a reaction to the way --- reacted?

Finally, group-as-a-whole processing questions are intended to help members learn about group dynamics and how they operate within groups. For example:
- What did you notice about how the group interacts?
- How will conducting this activity affect the group's functioning?

The group leader utilizes processing to facilitate one or more of the therapeutic factors as the result of the activity. Yalom (1995) emphasized that simply experiencing events (or activities) in a group is not sufficient to facilitate change. Rather, an examination of the experience (or processing) is necessary to be able to retain, integrate and generalize these experiences.

Shechtman (2007) reviewed the application of Yalom's (1995) therapeutic factors to children and adolescents in groups. While results differed by the type of measurement used, several factors were identified as being important. These include **cohesion, catharsis,** and the **development of socializing techniques/skills. Interpersonal learning, altruism, universality** and **instillation of hope** have also been identified as beneficial. In psychoeducational groups, **imparting of information (guidance)** and **imitative behavior (vicarious learning)** may be of particular importance (Delucia-Waack, 2006).

Processing facilitates **cohesion;** as group members are invited to engage interpersonally with one another in more meaningful ways, a sense of belonging to the group results. Processing can also be used to facilitate **catharsis** by encouraging the expression of group members' emotional reactions to an activity. When group members are invited to relate interpersonally with each other and practice or review specific social and interpersonal skills, the **development of socializing techniques** occurs.

By engaging students in processing, they are encouraged to learn about themselves and one another, which facilitates **interpersonal learning. Altruism** results when students find that sharing their own experiences also allows them to assist others. When common reactions are identified and new ideas discussed, **universality** and **instillation of hope** develop.

Activities that are used to teach specific skills can be followed by processing questions about what students learned, how they learned it, and what has prevented them from utilizing this skill in the past. Such questions facilitate **imparting of information, or guidance.** Finally, as students observe others gaining new patterns of thoughts, feelings, or behaviors through the processing of activities, **imitative behavior, or vicarious learning** can result.

Models of Processing

Kees and Jacobs (1990) identified three critical elements involved in processing activities: good questioning skills, advanced accurate empathy (Egan, 1986), and an awareness of the focus of the group with the ability to hold, shift, and deepen the focus (Jacobs et al., 1988). Good questioning skills involve using open-ended questions that help group members to develop new insights and awareness (Kees & Jacobs). Advanced accurate empathy involves being fully present for the client and mirroring and reflecting anticipated feelings and reactions that may be unstated or understated by the members themselves. For example, "You are saddened by the loss of your mother, and you fear that you will feel alone for a long time. It is difficult for you to hear the other members reaching out to you. The group though is supporting you right now." Empathy serves to communicate understanding and validation on interpersonal, intrapersonal, and group-as-a-whole level. It also serves to model empathy for members and facilitate cohesiveness.

Finally, Kees and Jacobs (1990) described the importance of awareness of the focus of the group with the ability to hold, shift, and deepen the focus. For example, "I'm hearing several issues. One is that time is in short supply right now. And there's also a frustration at not being able to give as much as you'd like to each of the areas of your life. Some of you seem to have some guilt about this."

It is important to note that the focus will differ according to the leadership and membership at any given point in time. For example, if there are two leaders, one of whom is more solution focused and one who is more interpersonally focused, they may seek to address different aspects of the process. Also, if there is a membership that is newer to "process," the focus will be on a more concrete level than on a more abstract level. In addition, contextual issues emerge. For example, in the aftermath of September 11th, existential issues may serve as a more relevant focus.

Hammell (1986) divided processing skills into concrete (knowledge, comprehension and application) or abstract (analysis, synthesis, and evaluation) thought processes. Concrete processing questions aim to review and describe events, feelings, thoughts, and problems. For example, "What were you feeling?" and "What did you see?" Abstract processing questions aim to identify patterns, make comparisons, relate learning to daily life, propose solutions, and examine values. For example, "How does this exercise relate to your life outside group?" and "What insights have you made about yourself?" This framework is based on Quinsland and Van Ginkel's

(1984) model that utilizes Bloom's (1956) Taxomony of Educational Objectives.

Stockton et al. (2000) also created a conceptual map to provide general guidelines for effective processing. Specifically, they conceptualize processing into four stages that are interrelated: identifying critical incidents of importance to group members, examining the event and member reactions, deriving meaning and self-understanding from the event, and applying new understandings towards personal change

Identifying critical incidents involves the group leader deciding what aspect of the process s/he will address. The group leader must ultimately use his/her empathic attunement to decide the "process direction," but Stockton et al. list some indicators that may help the leader make this choice. Examples of these indicators include heightened emotional or behavioral reactions from group members, conflict in the group, emotional self-disclosure, or body language that suggests unspoken reaction to an event/activity.

Examining the event and member reactions involves the leader engaging the group in a here-and-now discussion. Stockton et al. make several suggestions to help clarify reactions to critical incidents, including posing direct questions to members, encouraging members to address each other directly and the use of "I" statements.

Deriving meaning and self-understanding from the event involves helping group members apply the critical incident to their personal lives, interactions, and experiences. For example, a group member who is responded to empathically by a leader who s/he has just challenged may learn that despite his/her previous experience, authority figures will not respond with hostility to his/her questioning. Such insights that occur in the here-and-now of the group's life are often how real change begins to happen. Stockton et al. encourage group leaders to use feedback as a way of helping members see themselves as they are. Leaders also model giving and receiving feedback. Most importantly, when other members are not directly involved in the critical incident, it is important to engage them in a conversation in which they share their learning as a result of the incident.

Finally, **promoting change** involves helping members apply what they have learned in the here-and-now interactions of group to their everyday lives. Stockton et al. also suggested several strategies for promoting change, including journaling, members restating their goals and clarifying their learning, and role-playing.

Processing needs to be included from the outset of groups so that the leader(s) can model its' significance and teach members how to facilitate it themselves. One of the goals of the group leader is to discourage the group's initial tendency to rely on the leader and encourage the group to move toward more direct member-to-member interaction. Activities can be used to invite members to comment on group processes rather than looking to the leader for direction and answers. An example of such an activity in this book is George Leddick's activity *Who's the Leader*. This activity teaches and encourages students to observe group member behaviors and non-verbal communication. These skills can then be built on as the group progresses.

Matching the Goals of Processing to the Stage of Group

To be effective, processing needs to be tailored to a group's stage of development as well as to the needs of individual members. In schools, psychoeducational groups are quite common. According to Delucia-Waack (2006), psychoeducational groups proceed through three stages: an initial stage, a middle stage, and a termination stage.

In the initial stage, the primary tasks relate to getting to know each other, joining and entering the group, and learning norms and expectations. Anxiety is typically high given the newness of the experience and the apprehension of sharing in the group. Activities at this stage should provide structure to reduce anxiety, and offer safe ways of encouraging students to begin sharing and interacting. In this book, Melissa Luke's *Props in a Box* utilizes various everyday objects to encourage participation and help students begin identifying appropriate group rules. Janice DeLucia-Waack's *A Garden as a Metaphor for Change in Group* uses images from a garden to help students begin to identify their own strengths and areas for change through a fun and easily understood metaphor.

Processing questions that are appropriate for this stage of group development include "How did you feel sharing with the group?", "Was there anything that would have made you feel more comfortable?", and "Was there anyone you felt connected to during this activity?" Processing comments made during the initial stage should focus on members' feelings of safety and trust, and establish links, commonalities and themes among members.

In the **middle stage** of a group as members overcome their initial hesitance and anxiety, the group can move toward helping members to work on their individual goals. According to Delucia-Waack (2006) this stage is characterized by "...intense affect, increased self-disclosure, and an accelerated willingness to work on one's own issues." (p. 33). Early in this stage group members may go through some period of resistance or reluctance to fully participate; however, this period may not be as intense or conflictual as that in adult counseling groups. The major tasks of the leader during this stage are to facilitate an atmosphere where students feel safe enough to take risks and try out new behaviors, and to enable members to work effectively in the group to do so.

An example of an activity that could be used early in this stage is Elisabeth Liles' *The Write Words.* This activity encourages increased self-disclosure while providing a moderately safe structure in which to do so. Processing questions could be used to explore students' risk-taking in the group, and to address resistance by exploring anything that might be causing them to hold back. *A Stone's Life*, by Lamke and McWhirter, and *Who Am I?* by Carmen Salazar, are examples of activities in this book that could be used later in this stage to allow members to work on their goals in the group.

Examples of process questions at this stage to facilitate intrapersonal and interpersonal learning might include "What did you learn about yourself? "What did you learn about others?" "How did the group help you?" and "What was useful/not useful?" Questions that can facilitate "group-as-a-whole" learning might include "How did it feel when – reached out to you?" and "What did you need from the group? Did you get it?" Process comments might include validating member's feelings and their attempts to reach out to one another. Ideally, process comments at this stage will begin to come from members themselves as they have learned to emulate the leader's own process comments.

Finally, in the **termination stage**, the major task is disengagement. Activities should allow students to reflect on their learning in the group and identify how it can be applied to their lives outside the group, as well as to allow them to say goodbye to the group and to each other. For example, the *Rainbow Web* activity by MaryLou Ramsey allows students to reflect on and visually represent their own learning as well as to communicate how other members have helped them in some way. Jake Protivnak's *Family Feud* offers a fun way to review, reinforce, and practice what members have learned throughout a group.

As members contemplate leaving the group, process comments should relate to what they have learned, how or from whom they have learned it, and how they will apply the insights they have learned in the group to new situations outside the group.

<u>Summary</u>

Processing group activities is an essential aspect of effective group work. It is during processing that students reflect and learn about the effects of their thoughts, feelings and behaviors on their interactions; how their thoughts, feelings, and behaviors have been replicated in group interactions; and alternative ways of behaving, feeling, and thinking in the future. Processing enables members learn the skills to better understand themselves and their relationships in order to be more successful in school and in life.

References
Bloom, B.S. (1956). *Taxonomy of educational objectives*. London: Longman Group.

DeLucia-Waack, J. L. (2006). *Leading psychoeducational groups for children and adolescents*. Thousand Oaks, CA: Sage Publications.

Egan, G. (1986). *The skilled helper* (3rd ed.). Pacific Grove: CA: Brooks/Cole.

Hammel, H. (1986). How to design a debriefing session. *The Journal of Experiential Education, 9,* 20-26.

Jacobs, E., Harvill, R., & Masson, R. (1988). *Group counseling: Strategies and skills*. Pacific Grove, CA: Brooks/Cole.

Kees, N.L. & Jacobs, E. (1990). Working with groups: Conducting more effective groups: How to select, and process group exercises. *Journal for Specialists in Group Work, 15,* 21-29.

Quinsland, L.K., & Van Ginkel, A. (1984). How to process experience. *Journal of Experiential Education, 7,* 8-13.

Shechtman, Z. (2007). *Group counseling and psychotherapy with children and adolescents*. Mahwah, NJ: Lawrence Earlbaum Associates.

Stockton, R., Morran, D.K., & Nitza, A.G. (2000). Processing group events: A conceptual map for leaders. *Journal for Specialists in Group Work, 25,* 343-355.

Yalom, I.D. (1995). *The theory and practice of group psychotherapy* (4th ed.). New York: Basic Books.

Chapter 4
Quality, Integrity, and Ethics in School Counseling Groups
Louisa L. Foss & David Hermon

Few counseling modalities hold as much potential for both good and harm as group counseling. The social context provides opportunities for learning and growth unavailable in individual contexts. In group, universality counteracts feelings of isolation and the observation of others' growth trajectories inspires hope (Yalom, 2005). Students may use the group to observe and experiment with effective social skills. The safety of the group may provide a refuge for vulnerable students where they can experience support and encouragement.

Opportunity in group counseling, however, is accompanied by risk. These risks include ever-present threats to confidentiality, the exponential power of negative social influence, and the unpredictability of groups in action. More important still is the school counselor's ability to appropriately plan and implement an effective group. Finally, school personnel and parents must believe in the group process and provide the administrative support necessary for a counseling group that has quality and integrity.

The school counselor's commitment to safety in the group is paramount. Group dynamics should be harnessed and carefully shaped in a way that benefits members but does not cause harm to particular members or the group as a whole. The growing literature on efficacious group counseling practices provides a guide for directing beneficial group interventions and practices. The amassed knowledge on ethical group practices may serve as a foundation upon which creative and safe group interventions are built. In contrast, an over-reliance on intuition may lead to decisions influenced by cultural norms, political pressures, or rationalization (Cottone & Tarvydas, 2006). The amassed knowledge on ethical group practice may serve as a foundation upon which creative and safe group interventions are built. Consulting with professionals, remaining current with the literature and best practices, and adhering to professional codes, rather than relying on intuitive ethical decision-making is paramount.

The ASGW *Best Practice Guidelines* (1998) provide direction for ethical practice during group planning, performing, and processing. Applied to the school counseling setting, a number of best practices emerge as requiring additional attention and caution. These include providing sufficient time and energy for group planning and screening, seeking and maintaining competence in group leadership, maintaining confidentiality within the culture of the school, using group processes to promote social justice and monitoring group outcomes. Each of these areas will now be discussed in turn.

Pregroup Planning

The best-laid plans can be thwarted by a crisis, especially in a school atmosphere. So how can a school counselor be ready to lead an effective counseling group? Proper planning for group goals and activities, membership, and practical issues is critical. For example, a counselor may wish to focus on processing painful feelings related to bullying, but environmental factors such as uncomfortable chairs or extraneous noises may cause distraction. Thus, even mundane planning around the setting of the group is critical. Though it may be challenging to set aside other pressing tasks, it is important to consider both the therapeutic and practical aspects of preparation for a smooth and productive group.

Clear goals provide purpose and direction for group planning and implementation. Prior to the development of any counseling group, a needs assessment should be conducted. Uncovering student, school personnel, and parent needs not only helps provide necessary direction, but also enlists the support of important stakeholders. The data gathered in the needs assessment can then be used to help drive the development of goals, which should develop out of a true collaboration with the actual group members. With intentionality, the counselor links objectives with in-session activities to reflect the over-arching goals of the group. In contrast, a haphazard or poorly-planned group is unlikely to reach specific counseling outcomes.

Member Screening and Preparation

Screening potential members for their compatibility with the group's member composition and overarching goals is an important pregroup preparation (Clifford, 2004). Group counseling is not indicated for everyone. A most elementary definition of screening is the selection of members who will personally benefit from the group and be beneficial to the group (Corey, 2008). Failure to properly screen can result in group dysfunction or harm to individual members. At the least, students should possess a basic level of interpersonal skills, including the ability to empathize, for helping others, and trust, for allowing oneself to be helped. Students with interpersonal insensitivity, such as those with autistic spectrum disorders, antisocial traits, or severe anxiety may struggle to effectively cohere with the group.

Helpful guidelines for child and adolescent group member selection are provided by DeLucia-Waack (2006). For example, students who are very different from the group should not be included, so as to avoid group scapegoating. Siblings and those students who have a notable history of conflict should not be placed in the same group. Age and the emotional development level of each child should be taken into account. Further, DeLucia-Waack advises identifying at least one other group member who can serve as a role model for each incoming member.

Leadership Competence

Competence is developed through knowledge acquisition, skills practice, and supervision and feedback. In a school counseling setting, this competence is most likely to be developed through group co-leadership whereby a novice school counselor is paired with an experienced school counselor. Co-leadership has other benefits as well, including the division of work responsibilities (Page & Jencius, 2009). Finally ongoing efforts to increase self-awareness to uncover biases and blind spots, as well as consultation and professional development to assist counselors at every stage of development continue on their journey toward competence and beyond to excellence.

Confidentiality

In all group counseling settings, confidentiality is a core challenge. The obligation to maintain the confidentiality of information disclosed in session does not just belong to the group leader, but to each group member as well. In the schools, where students mingle and interact constantly in numerous unpredictable academic and social situations, maintenance of confidentiality is far more challenging than in other counseling groups. If another group member breaks confidentiality, either intentionally or accidentally, other group members could be seriously harmed..

The ASGW *Best Practice Guidelines* (1998) indicate that the limits of confidentiality should be clearly communicated prior to the beginning of the group. Preferably, this process should occur during screening or pregroup preparation and then again at the beginning of group. In addition, the group counselor may remind members of confidentiality at various times throughout the group's existence, especially when sensitive topics are discussed. Thus group members are more likely to be aware of the potential costs associated with sharing personal information as well as the responsibility for maintaining others' information.

Social Justice

As school counselors, the empowerment of marginalized students should be a top priority (Stone, 2005). The school counseling group can either help or hinder this process. As Yalom (2005) indicated, the group typically serves as a social microcosm, or reflection of the individual's larger social world. As such, social power structures and hierarchies tend to replicate themselves in the group setting. Counselors are not immune to these influences and may unintentionally harm individual group members or the group as a whole by playing out biases. These dynamics may be ignored or the group can be used as an opportunity to combat social inequities. Further, the work of the school counselor and the groups within the school can serve to enrich the larger school environment by appreciating and honoring diversity.

Outcomes Assessment

While there are numerous formal outcomes assessment instruments for group work, it is not necessary for school counselors to engage in complicated assessment. Simple but intentional strategies for monitoring the group process and individual members' progress toward goals can be highly effective. Perhaps most important is acquiring a reflective stance that constantly compels the group counselor to consider "What can be done to improve this group?"

Delucia-Waack (2006) provides a number of guidelines for acquiring both positive and negative feedback from group members. Counselors are advised to collect outcome data not just from the student group member, but from multiple sources such as parents and teachers. Data should be collected at various times throughout the group process, as well as several months after the group to check for retention of progress. An instrument identified or developed during pregroup preparation can be integrated into group activities, perhaps as a check-in or check-out ritual. In addition to these guidelines, it is important that the identified outcomes link back to goals, objectives, and activities in a seamless and intentional manner. These outcome data are then easy to use in improving ongoing or future groups. Further, the data may be used to justify the existence or expansion of group counseling programming in the increasingly resource-limited school environment.

References

ASGW (1998). From the Association for Specialists in Group Work: Professional standards for the training of group workers. *Journal for Specialists in Group Work, 24,* 7-14.

Clifford, M. W. (2004). Group counseling and group therapy in mental health settings and health maintenance organizations. In J. L. DeLucia-Waack, D. A. Gerrity, C. R. Kalodner, and M. T. Riva (Eds.), *Handbook of group counseling and psychotherapy.* (pp. 414-426). Thousand Oaks, IL: Sage.

Corey, G. (2008). *Theory and practice of group counseling* (7th ed.). Pacific Grove, CA: Brooks/Cole.

Cottone, R. R., & Tarvydas, V. M. (2006). *Counseling ethics and decision-making* (3rd ed.). Upper Saddle River, NJ: Prentice Hall.

Delucia-Waack, J. L. (2006). *Leading psychoeducational groups for children and adolescents.* Thousand Oaks, CA: Sage.

Page, B. J., & Jencius, M. J. (2009). *Groups: Planning and leadership skills.* Boston, MA: Lahaska Press.

Stone, C. (2005). *School counseling principles: Ethics and law.* Alexandria, VA: American School Counselor Association.

Yalom, I. D. (2005). *The theory and practice of group psychotherapy* (5th ed.). New York: Basic Books.

Chapter 5
Effective Collaboration with School Personnel And Other Stakeholders
Judy Green & Wendy Fragasse

In addition to the students involved, a key element to the success of any school group depends largely on the school counselor's relationship with outside support. Support must include parents, administrators, and teachers as well as all other school support staff. Just as cohesion among group members is essential for an effective, productive group (Yalom, 2005), so is a positive connection to sources beyond the school counselor. For group work to be accepted and championed as the efficient, effective modality that it can be, the school counselor must reach out to all stakeholders and strive to bring everyone involved into a collaborative arrangement (Erford, 2003).

Because group work at times necessitates students' removal from the classroom setting, school counselors must be sensitive to the academic implications and other possible variables that impact a successful school group. Indeed, recent research indicates that support from administrators, teachers, and parents plays an important role in school counselors' ability to establish and run groups in the school setting (Steen, Bauman, & Smith, 2007).

Administration

As with any program implemented in a school, approval from the administration is essential. In order for groups to be effective, it is the school counselor's responsibility to ensure support and collaboration by establishing a cooperative relationship with school administrators through the maintenance of ongoing, open dialogue regarding all counseling programs including the running of any type of group (Greenberg, 2003). Research has shown that the establishment of a positive working relationship with school administrators is vital to school counselors' success in carrying out their myriad of duties (Niebuhr, Niebuhr, & Cleveland, 1999). The school administrators, including the building principal and district superintendent, must have a clear understanding of the target population, the rationale for the group, the group process and goals as well as the logistics (time, place, materials, duration) necessary to facilitate each group (Greenberg, 2003).

The first step in this process is to define and determine the need for whatever type of group is being offered. There are a number of ways to determine this, e.g., including, but not limited to, staff input, needs assessments, simple surveys, as well as current research and trends. Other data easily accessible to the school counselor include discipline referrals, attendance records, teacher or parent referral, or results of standardized tests. When formulating group topics, these records offer baseline data which in turn can be collected again later and used to show progress in measurable ways, e.g., fewer absences, higher test scores or subject grades, and fewer discipline referrals or school suspensions (Hardesty & Dillard, 1994).

Once the topics for the groups are established, the next step is to provide the administration with a concrete plan which should include all of the elements described in previous chapters, such as the purpose/rationale for the group, type of students who will be invited to this group, how the selection process will take place, the duration of the group, permission forms, and materials. The school counselor's authority as the group leader to admit or deny participation to individual students is essential to the effectiveness of any group success. By including administrators in this fundamental step, counselors have the opportunity to strengthen the administration's confidence in the counselor's ability to run each group independently from member selection to the conclusion of the group process. Once approved by the administration, the school counselor will be prepared to approach teachers and support staff with the proposal of running groups during the school day as well as to ask for referrals of potential group members.

Teachers

School counselors must have a good working relationship and the support of teachers for group success (DeLucia-Waack, 2006). Teachers are a valuable source of referrals to the school counselor for students who may be in need of individual or group counseling. By including teachers as part of the team of professionals working together to improve the overall academic success of all students, the school counselor will improve cooperation and lessen resistance in the important effort to establish and maintain groups. As early in the school year as possible, the school counselor needs to educate the faculty regarding the necessity for and the types of groups that may be run throughout the academic year.

In order to help minimize class disruption and further demonstrate that the school counselor appreciates the teachers' willingness to accommodate a student's need for group participation, teachers must be included in a pre-group meeting to discuss the goals and objectives of the group, the selection of group members, and a possible schedule for the group to meet. School counselors are not only asking for flexibility when removing a student from class for group participation, but also for support by the teachers for the group members both academically and emotionally when they return to class following group. Regular and ongoing communication with the teaching staff is vital in order to fully understand group members and their needs.

Once groups are ongoing, while respecting group members' confidentiality, it is beneficial to offer teachers regular, general feedback on any relevant issues that may be impacting a student's wellbeing or success regarding academic or behavioral classroom performance. Likewise, teachers must be asked to inform the school counselor of observed student behaviors or attitudes in the classroom, whether positive or negative. This communication reinforces the importance of mutual respect and collaboration between the school counselor and teachers, thus maximizing benefits to the students in the group (O'Day, 2002).

Teachers' assistance is also beneficial to the group process in terms of record keeping, data collection, and measurement of progress. School counselors can request that teachers administer a pretest before a group begins, a posttest immediately following the termination of a group, and a follow-up post test a few months later. Sharing and discussing the results of this type of collected data with teachers as well as administrators will demonstrate how participants have changed through group involvement as well as reinforce the school counselor's role as a member of the team of professionals working together to increase student success (Steen et al., 2007). Analysis of available data can serve as a springboard to discuss ways to improve group performance in the future, brainstorm ideas for new types of groups, or determine how a certain group may be run differently to have a more positive impact on student success.

<u>Support Staff</u>

Cafeteria workers, bus drivers, monitors, secretaries and custodians are just a few who make up the support staff in any school. Many times these personnel have a unique and keen awareness of the students in the school. They often observe students in unstructured, more social settings versus the more formal classroom settings as seen by teachers, counselors, or administrators. Due to the nature of these settings, many issues surface which might go unnoticed without input from these key people.

Additionally, support staff might be in a position to assist with alternate discipline measures when appropriate. For example, a member of a group of at-risk students might be permitted to work with a custodian or cafeteria worker during a free period or study hall rather than serve an after-school detention. The school counselor's ability to foster this type of collaboration has the potential to include all school employees as partners in the school counseling program, an effort that will enable students to build positive relationships with others in the school while simultaneously increasing the school counselor's credibility as one who is indeed part of a team working for the success of all students (Stone & Dahir, 2006).

<u>Parents</u>

Parents have significant influence and power over their children (Stone & Dahir, 2006). This dynamic may obviously have either positive or negative components. It is in the students' best interests that school counselors are not only aware of these relationships, but also actively seek the involvement of parents as much as possible in the group process. Involving parents in this manner lets them know that they are valued as an essential part of the team working to improve their child's success in all school related areas.

It is important to keep in mind that it may be difficult to obtain parental agreement for their children missing class time to work on non-academic issues. Too often, parents hear only bad news from the school. Positive messages from the school counselor or any school personnel go a long way in building bridges with parents. Letting parents know whatever success their child has gained from involvement in a group process can serve not only to further promote the group process in the future but also may improve parental interaction with their child. This, in turn, may have positive outcomes in terms of the student's self-esteem as well as improved academics (Steen et al., 2007). Therefore, it is the school counselor's responsibility to educate parents of the importance of the areas to be addressed in a small group and how their child's involvement would be linked to positive academic and personal growth.

Sharing the Excitement

School counselors who currently run groups need no convincing that group work is an exciting, efficient, productive modality by which to impact students and bring about positive change. However, enthusiasm for group work does little good if it is not shared by the stakeholders of the community. If others do not understand or appreciate the unique strengths of group counseling in the schools, resistance can quickly and easily ruin the best efforts.

In response, the proactive counselor should seek to inform, educate, and excite others about the potential for student growth through counseling groups. Promoting group work and its advantages will help others to get on board and will help the counselor maintain his or her own passion in this process. Not only do students thrive in the group process, so do counselors who believe in their work.

References

DeLucia-Waack, J.L. (2006). *Leading psychoeducational groups for children and adolescents.* Thousand Oakes, IL: Sage.

Erford, B. (2003). *Transforming the school counseling profession.* Upper Saddle River, NJ: Pearson.

Greenberg, K. (2003). *Group counseling in k-12 schools: A handbook for school counselors.* Boston: Allyn & Bacon.

Hardesty, P.H., & Dillard, J.M. (1994). Analysis of activities of school counselors. *Psychological Reports, 74,* 447-450.

Niebuhr, K.E, Niebuhr, R.E, & Cleveland, W.T. (1999). Principal and counselor collaboration. *Education, 119,* 674-678.

O'Day, J. (2002). Complexity, accountability, and school improvement. *Harvard Educational Review, 72*(3), 293.

Steen, S., Bauman, S., & Smith, J. (2007). Professional school counselors and the practice of group work. *Professional School Counseling, 11,* 1096-2409.

Stone, C., & Dahir, C. (2006). *The transformed. school counselor.* New York: Lahaska Press.

Yalom, I.D. (2005). *The theory and practice of group psychotherapy (5th ed.).* New York: Basic Books.

Activities
for Children

Holding Hands:
Teaching Children How To Find Support
Submitted by Michael Lamke and Paula T. McWhirter

Goals:
- ✓ Develop interpersonal skills
- ✓ Recognize and respect differences in various family configurations
- ✓ Use effective communication skills
- ✓ Learn that communication involves speaking, listening, and nonverbal behavior

Target Population: Ages 9-13
Appropriate students for this activity are those who are experiencing difficulties feeling emotionally supported through changes in their parents' relationship due to discord within or dissolution of the relationship.

Potential Stage/Session(s): Transition or working stage

Estimated Time Length: 30-45 minutes

Materials: DVD Video *The Story of Us*, Ch. 11, 50:11-51:24

Activity:
Showing and processing the video, *The Story of Us*, will help students understand that responding to changes in one's family can be very difficult. Specifically, *it is normal to feel scared, alone, angry, or sad.* This activity helps students accomplish the following:
- ✓ Identify that talking about our feelings with someone we trust is a good way to help us learn how to adjust to the changes in our families.
- ✓ Process the fact that attempting to fix our parents' relationship is a natural reaction because we feel more comforted when the things we depend on are working. When they are not working, we tend to feel anxious and scared.
- ✓ Process the reality that the child did nothing to make their parents' relationship hurt and that it is not the child's responsibility to fix their parents' relationship.
- ✓ Identify and process the fact that children remain loved, even if their parents are in conflict with each other or become divorced.

Specific Directions for Activity:
Allow the students to briefly discuss their awareness of their current family situation. Inform the students that they will view a video clip showing a girl whose parents are not happy in their marriage. The girl senses that something is not right in her parents' relationship, but she is unsure as to what exactly is wrong. Explain to the students that watching the video clip may create difficult feelings within them, such as sadness, anxiety, or fear. Play the video *The Story of Us*, Ch. 11, 50:11- 51:24

Processing Questions/Conclusion:
Process the video clip by asking questions from the following three clusters:
- ✓ What feelings did the girl in the video have? What told her that something was wrong between her parents? What did she do to try to help her feelings? Do you think her actions helped her feel better?

✓ How did you feel as you watched the video clip? How have you felt about the struggles your parents are experiencing in their relationship?
✓ Have you tried anything to help yourself feel better about your parents' struggles in their relationship? Did any of these things work?

Have the students brainstorm and explore ways that they can feel supported and more comforted as they attempt to adjust to the changes or struggles occurring within their parents' relationship. (Group leader(s) should assist this process as needed)

Cautions:
This activity requires that students identify and respond to personal feelings related to changes in their family structure. It is necessary to have an understanding of the level of comfort or adjustment that each individual has experienced in relation to changes in their family. Gaining parental permission to engage in this group activity with their children would be necessary. Providing information worksheets about the activity to parents describing the activity and offering advice for helping to support their child's adjustment is a good idea.

The movie is rated R. Much of the content of the movie is not appropriate for viewing with children. While there is no inappropriate content in the video clip used in the activity, it may be most prudent to obtain administrative approval prior to showing the video clip.

Credit/References:
Merriam-Webster's collegiate dictionary (10th ed.). (1993). Springfield, MA: Merriam-Webster.
Zweibel, A. (Producer), & Reiner, R. (Director). (2000). *The story of us* [Motion picture]. Hollywood, CA: Universal Studios.
Zunker, V.G. (2006) *Career counseling: A holistic approach.* (7th ed.). Belmont: Thomson Brooks/Cole.

About the Group Workers:
Michael Lamke is a licensed Marital and Family Therapist and currently practices in the Child and Family Counseling program at a community-based counseling center in Norman, Oklahoma.

Dr. Paula T. McWhirter is an Assistant Professor of Counseling Psychology at the University of Oklahoma.

Feelings of Anger
Submitted by Stephen Kennedy and Holly Kayler

Goals:
- ✓ Learn to label angry feelings
- ✓ Express anger in safe, adaptive ways

Target population: Ages 8-12

Potential Stage/Session: Any stage or session, but participants may benefit from learning these skills early in order to use them during the majority of group

Estimated Time Length: 30 minutes

Materials: Building blocks; one sheet of bubble-wrap for each group member

Introduction: Ask about each member's past experience with anger, such as:
- ✓ Can you think off a time when you felt angry?
- ✓ Do you remember what made you angry?
- ✓ What did you do about it?

Activity:
1) Invite the participants to think about something that makes them angry and start stomping their feet. Say, "When you feel your feet getting warm, that's the anger leaving your body." Tell students that they can continue stomping until they no longer feel angry.
2) Tell students that they will each build a tower of blocks. Instruct the student to place a block down and identify something that makes them angry; repeat until the student has built tower to desired height. At this point, ask the child to say (or yell, if the room is soundproof) "I hate... [whatever he/she hates]!" and knock down the tower.
3) Distribute bubble-wrap and tell students that they can also release anger by squeezing a bubble between their thumb and fore-finger. Say, "a little bit of anger is released when you pop a bubble, and you can keep going until you are no longer angry." Also, tell students when they are really anger they can squeeze many of the bubbles at once to release more anger.

Processing Questions:

- ✓ Could you feel the anger leaving your body?
- ✓ What did it feel like?
- ✓ How did your body feel when the anger was out?
- ✓ Which of the three activities worked best for you?
- ✓ In the future, what can you do when you feel angry? What can you do besides these activities?

- ✓ How can you release anger in a quiet way?
- ✓ Can you think of some safe places for releasing anger?

✓ Can you think of some unsafe places for releasing anger?
✓ In the future, where might you choose to release your anger?

Cautions:
These activities can be noisy, so it is advisable to conduct them in a soundproof room or a place where other groups or classes are not nearby.

Credit/References:
Saxe, S. (1997). The angry tower. In H. Kaduson & C. Schaefer (Eds.). *101 Favorite Play Therapy Techniques* (pp. 246-250). Northvale, NJ: Aronson.

Wunderlich, C. (1997). Stomping feet and bubble popping. In H. Kaduson & C. Schaefer (Eds.). *101 Favorite Play Therapy Techniques* (pp. 283-285). Northvale, NJ: Aronson.

About the Group Workers:
Stephen Kennedy is a second-year master's counseling student at the University of North Carolina-Greensboro.

Holly Kayler is a Licensed School Counselor and doctoral student at the University of North Carolina-Greensboro.

Who's the Leader?

Submitted by George R. Leddick

Goals:
- ✓ Increase powers of observation
- ✓ Improve sensitivity to nonverbal communication

Target Population: Ages 6-10

Potential Stage/Session(s): Orientation stage/ First, second, or third session

Estimated Time Length: 20 minutes for 20 people (Duration may be modified depending on number of guessers)

Materials: Sufficient space for circle of chairs (alternative: sit on floor or stand)

Activity: A volunteer leaves the area while the group selects a leader. The leader's job is to lead the group in a series of sequential nonverbal motions (twiddling thumbs, leaning on left hand, leaning on right hand, snapping fingers, waving, tapping feet, big frown, big smile, clapping, eyebrows up, eyebrows down, etc). The leader tries to hide his or her identity from the volunteer. The person who is "It" gets three guesses to name the leader.

Specific Directions for Activity:
Everyone move your chairs into a circle! We are going to play a game called *Who's the Leader?* Who would like to volunteer to guess first? Carmen? Okay, stand right outside the door and we will come get you in just a minute.

Now we need a leader for this group, Dale? Okay, here's Dale's job. Dale must switch from one motion to the next, never stopping. And every time Dale changes, the rest of the group copies, just like Simon Says. You can make any motion you like, but nobody can talk! You could lean on one hand, give a big frown, snap your fingers, or tap your feet. Watch me do it and copy what I do (demonstrates). See if you can think of new motions. But the leader is trying not to get caught. Carmen will get three guesses to find the leader. Okay, let's see the group get going. Watch your leader, but not always! Make it hard to guess! I'll go get Carmen, so get warmed. up.

Okay, Carmen. Here is the group. They will switch the motions they make. They have a secret leader. You have 3 tries to guess who it is. Watch for the changes.

At the end of three guesses, the leader is revealed and a new volunteer gets a turn to guess.

Processing Questions/Conclusion:

- ✓ We had 4-5 people guess the leader, what did they do to make their guesses?
- ✓ How did you make it hard to guess the leader? How were you sneaky? Where did you look?

✓ Were there any new motions? Which ones did you like? Were they big motions or little motions? Is it harder when you mix them?
✓ Is it easier to watch faces or motions? What makes it easy?
✓ I like the way you were all increasingly observant. You are getting good at this game!

Cautions:
The first few people who are "It" making guesses should be among the most capable in the group so they can model for the others. Do not choose unpopular children for the initial round, to avoid scapegoating and exclusion.

Credit/References:
I learned this game in 1958 from my 5th grade teacher Mrs. Howe (formerly Miss Smith) at Perry Hall Elementary School in Baltimore, MD.

About the Group Worker:
Dr. George R. Leddick is a Counselor Educator, a former ASGW Past-President, and a Fellow of the Association for Specialists in Group Work (ASGW).

I Am Special

Submitted by Monica Hunter, Joel Lewis and Andre Green

Goals:
- ✓ Identify positive characteristics in themselves
- ✓ Gain the ability to understand how to address negative feedback from others
- ✓ Recognize and accept themselves by focusing on their own positive characteristics and understanding how they are special

Target population: Ages 6-10
This activity is especially helpful for students dealing with self esteem issues

Potential /Session(s): Orientation stage

Estimated Time Length: 30 minutes

Materials: White art paper, construction paper, crayons, markers or colored pencils, a thesaurus, yellow stars, gray dots, *You Are Special* book by Max Lucado (The story discusses the negative interactions Wemmicks have with each other and how the main character goes through the process of overcoming negative feedback.)

Activity: Tell the students that you are going to read a story today about a fictional town of wooden people called Wemmicks. Tell the students to think about how the story relates to real life. Read the story. Begin a discussion by asking the students the following questions: What is similar in this story to some of the things that happen in real life? Even though we don't really go around giving people dots, in what ways do we focus on people's faults? Give an example of some things you have heard. How did it make Punchinello feel when people gave him dots? How do you feel when people say negative things about you? Why didn't Lucia have any dots? What was the difference in Lucia's attitude and Punchinello's attitude when people said negative things about them? How did Punchinello start to lose the dots? How can we change our thinking about ourselves to make sure we don't ever have "dots?"

Specific Directions for Activity:
Pass out one gray dot and one yellow star to each group member. Tell the students to listen to the statements the group leader will read and ask them to think if the statement fits a gray dot attitude or a star attitude. After the group leader reads the statement the students will hold up a gray dot or a star to fit the attitude of the statement. Read the following statements: She is ugly, I am no good at anything, I will try my best, He's stupid, If I believe, I know I can achieve, I believe in myself. Tell the students you want them to develop "star attitudes." Start by having them thinking about some special things about themselves. Some of them are special because they like to help others, some of them are kind, etc.

Tell the students you want them to create a concrete portrait of themselves. First, give them the white sheet of art paper and crayons/colored pencils for them to draw a portrait of just their faces. Explain that the portrait should be large (as if they were holding a mirror up to their face). Next, have the students brainstorm a list of positive words to describe themselves (You can have a thesaurus on hand to help students build their self-esteem vocabulary). Finally, have the students write the words on the outer edge of their portrait, so the words begin to take the shape of their portrait (the words should curve around their hair, etc.).

Processing Questions/Conclusion:
✓ Invite students to share their portraits with the class
   Ask members to comment on how each portrait is unique or how the portraits are similar

✓ Why is it important for you to know you are special?
✓ Are there times when you find it hard to remember that you're special?
✓ How does this activity remind you that you are special?

Cautions:
The book could have some religious/spiritual undertones. How would this be a problem? One of the characters is the woodcarver. He is also referred to as "the maker" of the wooden people in one section of the book. This book is absolutely wonderful and children of all ages enjoy it.

Credit/References:
Lucado, M. (1997). *You are special.* Wheaton, IL: Crossway Books.

About the Group Workers:
Monica Hunter, Ph.D., is a former elementary and secondary School Counselor and Counselor Educator at the University of South Alabama.

Joel Lewis, Ph.D., is the director of the Mobile Youth Leadership Program and an Assistant Professor in Instructional Design and Development at the University of South Alabama.

Andre Green, Ph.D., is a former secondary science teacher and works as a Professor in secondary science at the University of South Alabama.

Are You Growing Worries?

Submitted by Amy Campbell

Goals:
- ✓ Understand the connection between thoughts and feelings
- ✓ Help students to identify ways they may perpetuate or stunt the growth of unpleasant feelings such as worry
- ✓ Discover specific coping skills for controlling worry
- ✓ Develop a perspective of empowerment over worry and other unpleasant feelings

Target population: Ages 6-10
This activity is helpful for students experiencing mild to moderate anxiety

Potential Stage/Session(s): Orientation stage/Second or third session of the group. It is important to do this activity at an early stage in the group because it facilitates responsibility with the students in handling their own anxiety. This sets the norm for them to be the active participants in the handling of their emotions while giving them a sense of empowerment verses powerlessness.

Estimated Time Length: 30-35 minutes

Materials: Small Potted Plant/Seed, The book *What to Do When You Worry Too Much* by Dawn Huebner (ISBN 1-59147-314-4)

Activity: All students will receive a plant. The group will have an open discussion about things they have grown in their lives, how you can get things to grow (taking care of it, paying attention to it, watering it, etc.) Be sure to focus on how, if you keep paying attention to it, a seed or a plant has the potential to grow and grow.
Then ask for feedback about how the group thinks this relates to worries.

Specific Directions for Activity:
Members read aloud Chapter One in *What to Do When You Worry Too Much*: Are You Growing Worries? Students are asked to discuss some worries that they have helped grow and those worries they were able to keep from growing.

Processing Questions/Conclusion:
- ✓ What do growing a plant and growing a worry have in common?
- ✓ How are growing a plant and growing a worry different?
- ✓ What can you do to keep a worry from growing and growing?
- ✓ What have you learned today about growing worries?
- ✓ How do you feel about the fact that you can help a worry grow or help stunt the growth of a worry?

Cautions:
It is important to know the origins of anxiety before placing students in a group or conducting an activity of this nature. The members of this group had anxiety surrounding their irrational beliefs. I gathered a wealth of information and met with the students on an individual basis before placing them in this group. Anxiety could be

a manifestation of something deeper and/or harmful that has occurred or is occurring in their lives.

Credit/References:
Huebner, D. (2005). *What to do when you worry too much: A kid's guide to overcoming anxiety.* Washington, DC: Magination Press.

About the Group Worker:
Amy Campbell is a former elementary School Counselor and current doctoral student in the Counselor Education program at the University of Virginia.

RAP (Repeat and Practice) Up Social Skills

Submitted by Marie Horton, Amber Lange and Amy Brown

Goals:
- ✓ To assess social skills competence acquired by at-risk students who have been participating in a social skills group.
- ✓ Help school counselors target social skill areas that are in need of continued improvement.
- ✓ Provide students with opportunities to practice steps and strategies necessary to develop targeted social skills.
- ✓ Provide students with opportunities to generalize social skills.

Target population: Ages 8-12
Cognitive abilities: 2nd grade or higher reading/comprehension level

Potential Stage/Session(s): Working stage

Estimated Time Length: 45 minutes

Materials: Game cards (made by the school counselor), die, play money (made by the school counselor or utilized from another game)

Activity:
This activity focuses on self-control and cooperation skills in a social context. Prompts are written on small, color-coded, rectangular cards and are used in this fun, engaging game.

Pre-group Preparation:
Draw business card-size rectangles onto a landscape sheet of white paper. There should be a total of 12 rectangles on a sheet. Based on group discussion of learned social skills, write a problem in each rectangle that can be solved by utilizing one of the social skills taught. Problems should be separated into self-control skills and cooperation skills.

Photocopy the sheet of self-control problems on one color of cardstock and photocopy a sheet of cooperation problems on a different color of cardstock. Assign each skill either an even or odd number. Cut out cards and place each card in either the even pile and the odd pile. Both piles should have problems that require self-control skills and cooperation skills. Utilize play money from another game or copy an additional sheet of rectangles. Assign each rectangle the value of one dollar.

Specific Directions for Activity:
Players roll a die and select from the color-coded category assigned to an even or odd number rolled on the die. Players select a card from the top of the matching pile and follow the instructions on the card. Cards require players to resolve a problem alone or by asking a peer for assistance. The school counselor should guide the decision making process. Each time a player uses skills learned in the social skills group to resolve the problem he or she collects one dollar. The first player to collect five dollars wins the round.

The RAP Up game provides meaningful opportunities for students to exercise target social skills learned in group. The game can be tailored to meet the specific needs of the group by changing the card instructions.

Processing Questions/Conclusion:
- ✓ What might be the best way to solve this problem?
- ✓ Can you think of another way to solve this problem?
- ✓ Who might you be able to ask for help?
- ✓ Does anyone in the group have a suggestion for how we could solve this problem?
- ✓ How could cooperation be used to solve this problem?
- ✓ How could you utilize self-control skills to solve this problem?

Credit/References:

Gresham, F. M. (2002). Social skills assessment and instruction for students with emotional and behavioral disorders. In K. L. Lane, F. M. Gresham, & T. E. O'Shaughnessy (Eds.), *Interventions for children with or- at risk for emotional and behavioral disorders* (pp. 242-258). Boston: Allyn & Bacon.

Lane, K.L., Givner, C.C., & Pierson, M.R. (2004). Teacher expectations of student behavior: Social skills necessary for success in elementary school classrooms. *The Journal of Special Education,* 38, 104-110.

Miller, M.J., Lane, K.L., & Wehby, J. (2005). Social skills instruction for students with high-incidence disabilities: A school-based intervention to address acquisition deficits. *Preventing School Failure,* 49, 27-39.

About the Group Workers:

Marie Horton, M.A., is a special education teacher in Toledo, Ohio and is currently completing a master's degree in Counseling at Spring Arbor University in Michigan.

Amber Lange, LPC, is a licensed counselor in Michigan and doctoral candidate in the Counselor Education program at the University of Toledo in Ohio.

Amy Brown, M.A., FS, is a high school teacher and current student in the Community Counseling program at Spring Arbor University in Michigan.

Millions of Families
Submitted by Bengu Erguner-Tekinalp

Goals:
- ✓ Recognize and respect differences in various family configurations
- ✓ Develop an awareness of differences and similarities of various types of families
- ✓ Demonstrate greater respect for different family configurations

Target Population: Ages 5-10

Potential Stage/Session(s): Orientation stage

Estimated Time: 30 minutes

Materials:
- ✓ Find different family pictures representing diverse family configurations from various ethnic/cultural groups.
- ✓ Copy of handout #1 *Sample Pictures of Families* for each student
- ✓ Copy of handout #2 *My Family* for each student
- ✓ Markers or crayons for each student

Activity:
This group incorporates sample family pictures to demonstrate the various family configurations of ethnic and cultural similarity and diversity. Art is used to engage students in developing insight, which is then used to stimulate group discussion and processing.

The school counselor opens the group by explaining that for this activity we will be looking at pictures of different types of families. Provide psychoeducation to the group on the various types of families: single-parent, some foster, adoptive, in some with two mothers, some families with two fathers, some are if different religions, some celebrate different holidays, etc. The school counselor may show different family pictures to the students and allow time to talk about each picture (see handout #1 *Sample Pictures of Families*. Students may be asked to share if they know some families who are like those in each picture.

In the second part of the group, students are invited to use markers or crayons to draw their own families on handout #2.

Processing Questions/Conclusion:

Each group member is invited to share their drawing with the group. During or after the sharing time, the following questions may be asked:

- ✓ What did you enjoy most about drawing your picture?
- ✓ Was it difficult to draw your family?
- ✓ Are there times when you feel like your family is very different from others'?
  - o If so, what is this like for you?

- ✓ Are there times when you feel confused or strange about the differences you see in others' families?
  - o Why do you think this is so?
  - o How can you change the way you feel when you see differences?
- ✓ How are our families in this group different? The same?
- ✓ What are some ways we can show respect for all the different families in our world?

Conclude group by emphasizing that all families have unique strengths. It is their job to find the strengths in their own and others' families and to respect the differences in the group and in their school.

Cautions:
The group leader should be sensitive to the children who are adopted or live in foster homes.

About the Group Worker:
Bengu Erguner-Tekinalp, Ph.D., is a Counselor Educator at the Drake University, Iowa.

Sample Pictures of Families
Handout #1

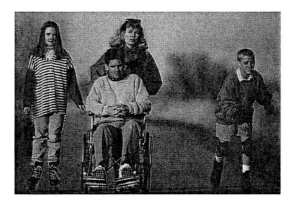

My Family
Handout #2

Name: _____

People First

Submitted by Zulema I. Suarez and Hugh C. Crethar

Goals:
- ✓ Learn to use correct terminology to refer to people with varying abilities, specifically the use of "people first" language
- ✓ Gain empathy skills regarding the use of labels when referring to other people

Target Population: Ages 9-11
This activity blends well with social skills groups.

Potential Stage/Session(s): Any stage or session

Estimated Time Length: 30-40 minutes

Materials:
- ✓ Pictures or depictions of people of all ages with different abilities,
- ✓ Two different labels for each picture
  Example: "Cripple" vs. "Person in a wheelchair"
- ✓ White board and dry-erase pens

Activity: People first language is language-use wherein the person is not described by the label, but instead as a person first followed by the label (whenever necessary). This group activity uses pictures or depictions of people with different abilities to teach group members to use people first language. Through this process, group members may gain sensitivity and increased levels of felt and expressed empathy.

Specific Directions for Activity:
Lead a brief discussion with the participants about diversity and different labels people use when they are not educated on the appropriate terms for people. Discuss with students how people often are given various labels because of how well they are perceived to fit in with what many label as "normal" in society. People often learn and use terminology that is intended to emphasize these variations or differences as something negative.

Ask the participants to think about what labels they have heard or used themselves to put each other down (e.g., crippled, invalid, gay, blind, handicapped, brain damaged, birth defect, deaf, retarded, etc). Be clear that they are to do this for a minute without calling out any of the labels.

Have the students discuss what labels they brainstormed. Write down the different ideas on a dry-erase board.

Show the participants pictures of people with apparent different disabilities and of various racial, cultural, religious, sexual, etc. backgrounds. Encourage students to think about what label they would give that person, without discussing it with anybody.

Give the students two different labels for each picture. Invite each student to choose an appropriate label for each picture. Once the students have chosen a label for each picture, have them share with the group which one they chose.

Discuss the answers and process reasons why some answers are preferable to others. Return to the dry-erase board with the answers that were discussed at the beginning, and replace the answers with the preferable terminology.

Processing Questions/Conclusion:
Throughout the group, the following questions may be used to prompt discussion:
- ✓ What kinds of names do people call you or someone you love that you think people should not use?
- ✓ How do you feel when people call you these names?
- ✓ How do you think people feel when other people call them the names we didn't leave up on the board?
- ✓ What are some names you will use more now that we have done this exercise?

Cautions:
Be sure to process the labels with the students, specifically if they have ever been called these names. Prior to the activity, it is important to emphasize the need for students to take turns talking, only share names and labels when called on, and talk in ways that are not hurtful to anyone in or out of the room.

About the Group Workers:
Zulema I. Suarez, M.Ed., is an elementary School Counselor in Tucson Unified School District.

Hugh C. Crethar, Ph.D., is a School Counselor Educator at the University of Arizona.

Hide in Sight
Submitted by George R. Leddick

Goals:
✓ Increase powers of observation and sensitivity to sound modulation

Target Population: Ages 6-10

Potential Stage/Session(s): Orientation stage/First, second, or third session

Estimated Time Length: 20 minutes for 20 people (Duration may be modified depending on number of guessers who serve as "It," or activity could be used again during a subsequent session.)

Materials: Kitchen timer, classroom with open traffic flow, any object (approximately as large as a big ring of keys, tennis ball, or a chalkboard eraser).

Activity: A volunteer hides his or her eyes. The group claps and makes noise (songs?) while an object is hidden in plain sight. The noise masks the footsteps of the hider. The person who is "It" stays seated and must locate the object. With younger children the counselor may wish to add hints of "you are hot" when looking near the object or "you are cold!" when looking on the opposite side of the room. After two minutes the kitchen timer dings, time is up and the object is revealed, then hidden by a new hider.

The person who is "It" can be selected by the counselor when there are members who struggle in handling the "It" role. The present "It" could automatically become the next one to hide the object. Decide ahead of time how you will handle selection of the hider and the "It." The counselor should select the first volunteer guesser, choosing someone who is friendly as a model for the others.

Specific Directions for Activity:
We are going to play a game called *Hide in Sight.* Who would like to volunteer to be "It" first? Dominic? Okay, Hide your eyes in your hands and no peeking until we say ready.

Now we need someone who can hide this eraser so it won't be noticed. But it has to be where we all can see it. Elyssa? Okay, Elyssa don't begin yet, just take some time to locate a sneaky hiding place. In the meantime, we all need to practice our cover-up noises so Dominic can't listen for footsteps. Let's clap like this! Okay! Now one more thing, clappers, you must NEVER look at the object once it is hidden. That's the hardest part! Okay, now keep up the clapping and Elyssa, it's time to HIDE IN PLAIN SIGHT!

Thanks Elyssa,(Counselor makes quieting signal*). Now that Elyssa is sitting down again, we must all be quiet enough to hear a pin drop! Shhhh! It's ok for Dominic to start hunting—start the timer!

At the end of 2 minutes the object is revealed and a new volunteer gets a turn to guess.

Processing Questions/Conclusion:

- ✓ When was it really hard to find the eraser? What made it difficult? Was it awkward because we were all looking at you?
- ✓ I kept forcing myself NOT to look at the eraser, was it hard for you too?
- ✓ Did anyone ever feel like they were hiding in sight or lost in a crowd?
- ✓ When you were looking for the eraser, what hints did you see in our faces?
- ✓ I like how observant you are getting. And you worked as a team: first you were noisy and then you were quiet! You are good at this game!
- ✓ What will you take away from this activity that will help you in school? With friends? In other situations?

* A quieting signal is a common technique in elementary school to regain quiet and focus on the counselor. Some counselors raise their hand, as each child notices they become silent, look at the counselor, and raise their own hand. Students try not to be the last hand raised. Alternately, counselors might briefly flick the lights off for attention.

Cautions:
The first few people who are "It" making guesses, should be among the most capable in the group so they can model for the others. The counselor should lead the group in clapping and in maintaining silence. When silence is broken, describe it as a difficult team effort to hold still (similar to freeze tag, where each child becomes a "frozen" silent statue). Being silent is a skill that requires lots of practice!

Credit/References:
I learned this game in 1958 from my 5ᵗʰ grade teacher Mrs. Howe (formerly Miss Smith) at Perry Hall Elementary School in Baltimore, MD.

About the Group Worker:
Dr. George R. Leddick is a Counselor Educator, a former ASGW Past-President, and a Fellow of the Association for Specialists in Group Work (ASGW).

Self-Esteem Sun Beams

Submitted by Aaron H. Oberman

Goals:
- ✓ Practice giving and receiving positive and encouraging words
- ✓ Begin to improve the self-esteem of group members

Target Population: Ages 6-12

Potential Stage/Session(s): Working or termination stage

Estimated Time Length: 30 – 45 minutes

Materials: white and colored construction paper (red, orange, yellow), scissors, glue stick or tape, and colored pencils or markers

Activity: This activity uses sun beams as a symbol for helping group members explore positive and encouraging words. An art activity assists students in delivering positive comments to other group members. Processing questions at the end of the activity help group members understand the importance of both giving and accepting positive statements.

Specific Directions for Activity:
The counselor may open the group with a definition of self-esteem and an explanation of the connection between self-esteem and sunshine.

For example, "Today we are going to work on an activity related to the sun. The sunshine is bright and usually linked to positive feelings and happiness. The more beams of light and encouragement group members receive, the better they will feel about themselves leading to increased self-esteem."

Depending upon the age level, the group leader may want to pre-cut the center of the sun and beams of light to cut-down on the time before beginning the activity.

- ✓ Give each group member a sheet of white paper and inner circle for their sun.
- ✓ Instruct the group members to write their name and one positive comment on the center of their sun.
- ✓ Have multiple sheets of colored construction paper (red, orange, yellow) available and ask the group members to cut out one sunshine beam per group member, and write their first name on the back of all the beams.
- ✓ Next, instruct the group members to share one of their beams with each group member.
- ✓ Then, instruct the group members to write a positive comment on each beam, and return all of the sunshine beams to the leader (the leader can inspect the sun beams to make sure all comments are positive).
- ✓ Last, the group members will glue or tape the center of the sun and the beams to the white sheet of paper.
- ✓ Ask the group members to share some of their positive comments received with one another.

Processing Questions/Conclusion:

- ✓ What was it like for you to give others in the group positive comments?
- ✓ How did you feel when you read your positive comments from the group members?
- ✓ Do you think it's harder to receive than to give a positive comment? Why or why not?
- ✓ Give an example of a time you gave someone a compliment or a time someone gave you a compliment that really meant a lot to you.
- ✓ Name one way you plan to encourage others this week.
- ✓ Name one way you will keep your own self-esteem sunbeams bright this week.

Cautions:

This activity works best near the end of a group or as a termination activity, so the group members have had a chance to learn more about one another throughout the group process. As noted earlier, it is a good idea for the group leader to review the sun beams before returning them to the group members, just in case someone gave another member a negative or otherwise inappropriate comment.

Credit/References:

Bowman, R. & Bowman, S. (2005). *Individual counseling: Lessons for adolescents.* Chapin, SC: Youth Light, Inc.

Jacobs, E. E., (1992). *Creative counseling techniques: An illustrated guide.* Odessa, FL: Psychological Assessment Resources, Inc.

Jones, A. (1998). *104 activities that build: Self-esteem, teamwork, communication, anger management, self-discovery, coping skills.* Richland, WA: Rec Room Publishing.

Studer, J. (2005). *The professional counselor: An advocate for students.* Belmont, CA: Thomson Brooks/Cole.

About the Group Worker:

Aaron H. Oberman, Ph.D., NCC, is an Assistant Professor of School Counseling at The Citadel.

Which Town Would You Choose?
Submitted by Bengu Erguner-Tekinalp

Goals:
- ✓ Learn to recognize, accept, respect and appreciate ethnic and cultural diversity

Target population: Ages 5-10

Potential Stage/Session(s): Orientation stage

Estimated Time Length: 30 minutes

Materials: A poster which has black and white pictures of towns/people who look unhappy, titled "Gray Town" and a poster made up of colorful pictures of towns/people who look happy entitled "Colorful Town."

Activity: In this activity participants will join in one thirty-minute lesson that will be delivered by the school counselor. The lesson consists of discussion about ethnic and cultural diversity. The students explore the importance of diversity by discussing two different imaginary towns.

Pregroup Preparation
Prior to the group, the counselor should create two posters. One poster in black and white, illustrates surroundings and families that are all very similar, without diversity. The second poster should be colorful, with numerous examples of social, racial, cultural, and religious diversity.

Hang the "Gray Town" poster on the board. Ask students the following questions:
- ✓ What kinds of things do you see in this town?
- ✓ How many colors do you see? Do people look happy in this town?

Hang the "Colorful Town" poster on the board. Ask students the following questions:
- ✓ What kinds of things do you see in this town?
- ✓ How many colors do you see?
- ✓ Do people look happy in this town?

Processing Questions/Conclusion:
- ✓ In which town would you like to live?
- ✓ Why?
- ✓ Does your neighborhood look like the first or the second town?
- ✓ How many different things do you see in your neighborhood?
- ✓ Do different families, people live in your neighborhood?
- ✓ How it might be if everything was the same.
- ✓ What is nice about having different cultures around us?
- ✓ How can different cultures enrich our neighborhood, our schools, our country and the world?

About the Group Worker:
Bengu Erguner-Tekinalp, Ph.D., is a Counselor Educator at Drake University, Iowa.

From Here to There

Submitted by Imelda N. Lowe and Virginia B. Allen

Goals:
- ✓ Increase group trust and cohesion
- ✓ Assist members in learning to work as a team
- ✓ Provide a safe environment for group members to learn how to work together

Target Population: Ages 8-11
This activity best serves students who struggle with trusting others

Potential Stage/Session(s): Working stage

Estimated Time Length: Approximately 30-45 minutes

Materials: One poster board cut in half for each team

Activity: This trust-building activity uses two poster boards cut in half and two teams that attempt to work together to move across the room without stepping off of the poster board. Prior to the activity, cut a poster board in half for each team or use two large pieces of heavy laminated cardstock. Ensure there is enough space in the room for students to move around freely.

Introduction to activity:
Ask the group why they think it is important for people to work together. Have the group discuss various situations where they have had to work with someone else. Explore their feelings about having to work with others, (for example: group assignments, team sports). Introduce the fact that sometimes people must work together to get a job done, such as in school with group projects, or in families where members help with chores.
After clearly establishing the fact that sometimes people must work together, introduce to the group that many times people must also trust each other. Have students define and explain "trust." Explore their feelings about being able to trust others.

Specific Directions for Activity:
After discussion, have the group divide into two teams. Have each team get on one side of the room. Let each team know that they will have to work together to complete the following activity.

Each team will have to get their team members to the other side of the room. Team members will use a poster board to cross the room and members may not step off of the poster board at any time while they are crossing the room. If team members step off of the poster board, they must start again. Once team members reach their destination on the other side of the room, they can get off the poster board; however, someone must remain on the poster board to return the poster board to team members on the originating side. The team who gets all their members to the other side of the room first wins.

Processing Questions/Conclusion:

Allow group members to discuss what it was like to work as a team. Explore the following questions with the group:

- What trust issues were experienced during the activity?
- How were the trust issues addressed?
- What do they think would happen if team members did not work together?
- How would that impact the team?
- What have you learned that you will you take from today's group?

Cautions:

Consider whether or not every student is physically able to participate. As this activity may require some physical contact, be aware of potential negative physical contact between team members.

About the Group Workers:

Dr. Imelda N. Lowe, LPC, NCC, is a Certified School Counselor and an Assistant Professor at The University of South Dakota.

Dr. Virginia B. Allen is a Professor of Counseling and School Counseling Program coordinator at Idaho State University.

Group Juggling
Submitted by J. Scott Glass

Goals:
- ✓ Learn at least one other person's name in the group
- ✓ Increase feelings of comfort within the group by laughing and having fun together
- ✓ Introduce group members to the process of effective problem-solving and goal setting

Target population: Ages 6-11

Potential Stage/Session(s): Orientation stage

Estimated Time Length: 15-20 minutes

Materials: 4 bean bags for up to 10 group members

Activity: Introduce the activity by asking, "How many of you can juggle (sometimes I let them show me)?" "If you were to pay to see a juggler, what is the one thing you do not want to see?" They answer, "Drops!" "Well, we are going to see how well we can juggle as a group."

Specific Directions for Activity:
The group stands in a circle. The leader then gives one bean bag to only one person. Let that person pick someone across the circle from him/her to throw it to, but call the person's name first, and then throw it underhand. If the person's name is not known, then have the individual ask the name. Now the next person should find someone across the circle that has not caught the bean bag and throw it in the same manner, calling his/her name and throwing it underhand. Do this until everyone has caught the bean bag and have the last person throw it back to the first person. This is now your pattern. Have the group practice going through the pattern another time or two so they become aware of where they are supposed to throw the bean bag each time it comes to them. They will always throw it to the same person for the entire exercise.

Once they have practiced a couple of times, hand out the remaining bean bags to various people in the group. Now say, "Go!" and have them start juggling with all of the bean bags introduced. You will notice that they will typically drop a number of them. Let this go on for a short time and then have them stop. Ask them, "How did we do since we were trying not to drop any bean bags?" Typically the answer will be, "Not good." Then the leader asks, "So what can we do to improve?" Have them share ideas and discuss what might and might now work. Then have them practice again while implementing some of their ideas.

Then you may give them the "30 Second Skills Test," which is simply saying "Go!," having them juggle for 30 seconds and then saying, "Stop!" The leader then goes around and counts up the drops of the group members. The leader then asks, "Can we improve on that number of drops?," or "Can we match that number again?" (if the group did not drop any the first time through). Again the group brainstorms regarding ways to drop fewer bean bags (i.e., better throws, etc.) and then tries the skills test once more.

Processing Questions/Conclusion:
✓ What was the hardest part of this challenge? Easiest?
✓ How did we as a group work through this challenge?
✓ How did we act towards each other during this activity?

✓ What role did you assume in the group during this challenge?
✓ What do you believe are the strengths and weaknesses of our group?
✓ How well does our group work together?
✓ How well is our group able to listen to one another and share ideas?
✓ What have we learned from participating in this challenge that will benefit us in our daily lives?
✓ What have we learned about working with others that will help us in other situations?
✓ What have we learned about ourselves that may affect how we handle other situations in the future?

Cautions:
Counselors must monitor that participants toss the bean bags underhand so as not to hurt one another. It is possible (and likely) that one group member may want to see how hard he or she can throw the bean bag and the group must be reminded of how they should throw to each other. In addition, counselors will want to pay attention to see if one person is the only one who consistently drops bean bags.

Often, if I notice that one person always drops the bean bags and nobody else seems to, I will include myself in the juggling and make sure that I miss some as well, so that the individual will not always stand out from the rest of the group members. Be aware of students who may find this task frustrating. If this is the case, use modeling to encourage other group members to support those who are struggling.

Credit/References:
Rohnke, K. (1984). *Silver bullets: A guide to initiative problems, adventure games and trust activities.* Dubuque, Iowa: Kendall/Hunt.

About the Group Worker:
Dr. J. Scott Glass is an Associate Professor in the Department of Counselor and Adult Education at East Carolina University.

Academic Success:
A Meta-Cognitive Approach

Submitted by Matthew E. Lemberger

Goals:
- ✓ Improve academic achievement in specific target areas
- ✓ Increase the immediate relevance and transferability between counseling services and the classroom curriculum

Target Population: Ages 8-11 with no more than one grade-level difference between students. Originally designed to target the "achievement gap" (i.e., focusing on student groups who traditionally score lower on standardized academic achievement measures, often in ethnically and economically marginalized populations), but useful for any student population.

Potential Stage/Session(s): Orientation or transition stage/ Second or third sessions

Estimated Time Length: Variable, typically 20 to 45 minutes.

Materials: Variable based upon the desired outcome of each session. Generally speaking, the school counselor should prepare lessons based upon preexisting school counselor standards in their respective state or district, using specific curriculum from the participants' classroom experiences, or research-supported activities that promote academic and school achievement. In the example lesson described below, students will only need a writing utensil and a blank piece of paper.

Activity: The example lesson described below is for students having difficulties with reading comprehension. The school counselor must consult with the English teacher in advance and glean the specific types of curricular content upon which the students are working in their respective classrooms. Additionally, the counselor must consult the teacher to target the specific areas of difficulties for each student, and then the counselor must embed the appropriate meta-cognitive learning interventions in the group activities. In this case, the students each struggle with identifying the "big ideas" in the text and how these concepts relate in terms of a larger narrative theme.

Specific Directions for Activity:

Introduction to Activity:

- ✓ To open the lesson, the group leader should check-in with each member regarding their respective mood, feeling, thoughts, and experiences since the last meeting. This check-in is designed to promote empathy, courage to disclose, and to provoke members to start cognitively tracking on their behaviors outside of the group. A great strategy for this check-in is to initiate a "go-round" using a scaling question (e.g., "Let's start with each of us taking turns stating a number 1 to 10 – one being a low feeling and 10 being a high feeling – to represent your mood or experiences this past week"). It is important to link experiences and emotions during and after the go-around.

✓ Next, the group leader should offer a brief review of the events and themes from the previous session. The purpose of this review is the highlight patterns that will be the bedrock for student schematic awareness, progress monitoring, and self-evaluation of growth.

✓ The final element of the lesson introduction is designed to affirm student investment and to demonstrate that group content will be framed. in terms of their values and desired outcomes. The group leader will ask the group to briefly report their goals, and then the leader will transition these goals into the preview of what will be the content of this particular group meeting.

   o An example goal-setting question and follow-up preview might be something like, "How would things be different if you could improve your reading comprehension skills?" and then, "It sounds as if the group is really motivated to make reading easier and more meaningful, well that's perfect because today's group assignment is to learn how to break stories down into small, manageable parts for easier understanding."

✓ The group leader will begin the activity portion of the group by discussing the importance of "prior knowledge" in learning. The leader will then explain this in more detail with a phrase similar to the following, "There are at least two types of prior knowledge that affect learning – how you feel about the activity, in this case reading, and what you know about the activity, in this case a story about how the pyramids were built."

   o "What are your feelings about reading, do you enjoy it or are it frustrating and, then, how do you think that these feelings affect your reading?"

   o "What specific things do you know about the construction of the pyramids?"

✓ The group leader will then process each of the responses with all members of the group and, when necessary, help correct misconceptions, encourage and reframe impeding feelings, and affirm accuracies and optimism.

✓ The group leader will read a short narrative passage (supplied by the students' classroom teacher). Then the group leader will ask the students to write what they believe are the five most important aspects of the story on the top of a blank piece of paper (e.g., "Choose what you believe are the most important aspects are the story. Use only one or a couple of words to represent these most important ideas."). At the same time, the group leader will write what she or he believes to be the five most important ideas on a separate paper.

✓ The group leader will then engage the group in a series of process questions. The purpose of these questions is to solicit group feedback, challenge the students to see different interpretations of the story, and facilitate students to become engaged in the process of meta-cognition (i.e., who she or he thinks about her or his thoughts). Example process questions include, but are not limited to the following:

   o "Who would be willing to share her or his five most important words and tell us why she or he chose those words?"

   o "Does anyone have anything to say about (name of peer student) five words?"

- o "Using these five words, what does this tell us about what the author was trying to say in this story?"
- o "Looking at your five words, can you rank order the most important aspects and the least important as they relate to what the author might have wanted to say in this story?"
- o "After listening to others in the group, are there any words that you might replace from your original list?"
- ✓ The group leader will conclude by asking the students to predict what might be her/his five items from the story. The leader will read the five items from her or his list and then ask inform the students of the logic behind these choices. The leader will then ask the following question, "If I were your classroom teacher, how might it be helpful to predict what I think are the important themes from a story?" The purpose of this question will be to trigger the students to consider the "expert learner" and to begin to predict what items might be on an exam.

Processing Questions/Conclusion:
The group leader will summarize some of the major aspects of the group session and highlight some of the important themes. More specifically, the leader will give names and definitions to the activities, for example:
- ✓ We started off by talking about how your feelings and what you know about something might affect how you understand a story that you read. This is called 'prior knowledge'.
- ✓ The process of choosing the five main ideas is called the "big ideas" in a topic. By identifying the most important ideas you can make a story easier to remember and it makes understanding how these ideas relate all the more handy.
- ✓ When we talked in the group, each one of you discussed how you think about your thoughts. This is important because this gives your ideas more meaning and it makes them more personal to you. It is easier to remember things that you have some personal connection with.
- ✓ Finally, when we compared answers, you practiced predicting what your teacher or what a test might ask you.

The group leader will then take each of the four aforementioned aspects and ask the students a series of process questions, for example:
- ✓ In what way might 'prior knowledge' affect your ability to answer a test, like for example when James said that reading frustrates him even before he starts to put his eyes to the words?
- ✓ How might you use the idea of 'big ideas' when you have a test or when you are taking your (insert the name of the state standardized test)?
- ✓ When reading a story, how can you ask yourself questions to make the story more meaningful?
- ✓ Before you read a story, how can you remind yourself to ask a question like, 'What questions might the teacher ask from what I am reading?'

The group leader will then ask the participants to first think about "the most helpful thing that you learned or re-learned from this lesson." Then the group leader will ask each participant to come up with a plan to work on this one lesson immediately after the group session has finished. Finally, the leader will instruct the participants to quickly write this idea and plan down on the sheet of paper and pair-share with a neighbor.

Finally, the group leader will preview the next session in one short sentence and offer the participants words of encouragement for each of their goals.

Cautions:
The students who are targeted for this group have often experienced numerous harmful messages and experiences in schools. When selecting group composition, the counselor should solicit members who have the potential to connect and work together and who can support an environment of respect and focus.

Although the intended design of this group is largely academic, it is important that the students enjoy the particular activities. Also, it is imperative that the activities are relevant to the school curriculum and that the school counselor work closely with the classroom teachers to reinforce the lessons learned in group.

Additional Comments:
School counselors should gather data relative to the students' achievement and in-school behaviors prior to, during, and after the close of the sessions. Using data to support the effectiveness of the intervention can be a pivotal marketing tool for future groups and the counselor's role in the school. Moreover, this data can inform the counselor of what is working in this group and what is not. The counselor, therefore, can adapt the group in future iterations to better service the needs of the students and school.

Credit/References:
Bransford, J. D., Brown, A. L., & Cocking, R. R. (1999). *How people learn: Brain, mind, experience, and school.* Washington, DC: National Academy Press.
Brigman, G., Webb, L., & Campbell, C. (2007). Building skills for school success: Improving academic and social competence. *Professional School Counseling, 10,* 279-288.
Lapan, R. T., Kardash, C. M., & Turner, S. (2002). Empowering students to become self-regulated learners. *Professional School Counseling, 5,* 257 - 265.
Webb, L., Lemberger, M. E., & Brigman, G. (in press). Students Success Skills: A review of a research based school counselor intervention influenced by Individual Psychology. *Journal of Individual Psychology.*

About the Group Worker:
Matthew E. Lemberger, Ph.D., is a former School Counselor and currently works as an Assistant Professor of Counseling and Family Therapy and School Counseling Programs Coordinator at the University of Missouri – Saint Louis.

We Live Under the Same Sky

Submitted by Bengu Erguner-Tekinalp

Goals:
- ✓ Learn to recognize, accept, respect and appreciate individual differences

Target population: Ages 5-9

Potential Stage/Session(s): Transition or working stage

Estimated Time Length: 30 minutes

Materials: Copy of *Poster 1*

Activity: The activity consists of observation of and discussion about different reactions to the individual differences. Ask students to arrange their chairs or sit on the floor in a circle. Explain to the students that you are going to show them a poster about the little camels playing on the playground at recess and that you are going to talk about what is going on in this picture. Hang the poster 1 on the board and let the students look at the poster. Explain that on the playground of the Big Forest Elementary School, the camels are playing on the playground. Three camels are playing together and one camel is watching them sadly. The three camels do not let the other camel play with them because he has only one hump.

Processing Questions/Conclusion:
- ✓ What is happening in this picture?
- ✓ Are all the camels alike?
- ✓ In what ways they are similar?
- ✓ In what ways are they different?
- ✓ How do you think the lonely camel feels?
- ✓ Is it okay to leave the camel alone just because he has one hump?
- ✓ How would you feel if you were left out?
- ✓ Have you ever felt left out?

Additional Comments:
This activity is designed as part of classroom guidance units to be implemented in comprehensive school guidance and counseling programs. This activity can be implemented in small or larger groups.

Credit/References:
Adapted from:
Page, P., Cieloha, D., & Suid, M (1990). *Intolerance. Getting Along: A program for developing skills in cooperation, caring for others, critical thinking, and positive conflict resolution. Teachers Guide.* Circle Pines, MN: American Guidance Service.

About the Group Worker:
Bengu Erguner-Tekinalp, Ph.D., is currently a Counselor Educator at the Drake University, Iowa.

My Roadmap

Submitted by Kara Ieva and Jacqueline M. Swank

Goals:
- ✓ Increase comfort in the group setting
- ✓ Recognize and understand that members are not alone in their foster/kinship care environment

Target Group: Ages 6-11; Children living in a either foster or kinship care

Potential Stage/Session(s): Orientation stage

Estimated Time Length: One group session 40-60 minutes

Materials: *My Roadmap* Worksheet

Introduction to Activity: Mention how all the members have something in common. They are all living in foster or kinship care, but all have been in different places.

Specific Directions for Activity:
1. Pass out *My Roadmap* Worksheet.
2. Explain to students that they will be asked to create a roadmap of their homes. The top of the worksheet states, "Where I got started," and the bottom states, "Where I am now."
3. Model a previously filled out one by the group facilitator.
4. Allow 5-10 minutes for students to create their roadmaps.
5. Ask students to share their roadmaps with the group.
6. As students are sharing, the facilitator can link similar stories.
7. Follow-up with process questions.

Processing Questions/Conclusion:
- ✓ Do you find your situation similar to anyone in the group? How?
- ✓ Has anyone ever felt the way _____ does? Or can you relate to anyone else in the group?
- ✓ Where do you see your roadmap going?
- ✓ Is it going in a direction you would like?
- ✓ What did you learn about someone in group today?
- ✓ What kinds of feelings were you experiencing when others were talking today?

Cautions:
If students cannot relate to someone else, they may be put off by group. Make sure that everyone is included on some level. Some may not want to share whose house they stayed in, so it is okay to use a nickname for the place they stayed.

Additional Comments:
This activity can also be used to focus on directions for future, such as jobs and plans for college with high school students.

Resource:

Durham, M. (2003). *Fostercare/ Kinship group.* Unpublished master's paper, Department of Education, Loyola College, Baltimore, MD.

About the Group Workers:

Kara Ieva, M.Ed., NCC, NCSC, is a doctoral student at the University of Central Florida in Counselor Education.

Jacqueline M. Swank is a licensed clinical social worker, registered play therapist and doctoral student at the University of Central Florida in Counselor Education.

MY ROADMAP

Where I started...

Where I am now...

Band-Aid Flipbook

Submitted by Monica Hunter and Shanell Petty

Goals:
- ✓ Understand the decision-making process
- ✓ Recognize and effectively handle peer pressure by making courageous decisions

Target population: Ages 8-11

Potential Stage/Session(s): Working stage

Estimated Time Length: 30 minutes

Materials: construction paper, plain white paper (optional), Crayons/ markers, Glue (optional), scissors, Pencil, Band-aids, "The Band-aid Chicken" book

Introduction to Activity: This activity discusses peer pressure and how it is not always easy to stand up and not go along with the crowd. This book uses cartoon illustrations of chickens to demonstrate this point, but it is extremely applicable to adolescents.

Activity: Ask the students if they had a choice between the following decisions which would they choose (have the students raise their hands): McDonald's or Burger King; Coke or Sprite.

Ask if they needed their friends to make these decisions (the response should be, no). Tell them that just like these simple decisions didn't require their peers, sometimes tough decisions will require you not to go along with your peers. The book you will read to them is about chickens and for them to reflect about what happens in real life that is similar to the book.

Read the story and discuss the following questions: What do you think made the chickens decide to peck the new chicken when they had gone through the bad experience before? Give examples of how this has happens in real life (in our society and with your friends)? Which chicken was more courageous? What do you think the Band-aid chicken was feeling before he stood up to the other chickens? Do we know of real people that are courageous decision makers like the band-aid chicken? Help students to identify and discuss courageous decision makers like Dr. Martin Luther King Jr., Rosa Parks, and incidents at their school, etc. How does this quote, "If not me, who? If not now, when?" relate to courageous decision making? Invite students to think of tough choices someone their age might currently face.

Give the students construction paper. Walk the students through the following directions for creating the flip book: Have students fold it in half vertically (the long way). Have students turn it horizontally and divide it into thirds (by cutting).

Directions for cutting: Opening the top half, students should cut until they come to the fold. Have students label the first third "Challenge." Then, the students can lift up the flap and draw a picture of the problem. Have students label the second third "Options." Then, students can lift up the flap and draw a picture of the options or write them. Have students label the last third "Choice." Then, students can lift up the flap and draw a picture of the courageous and positive choice that was made. In keeping with the theme of the book, the counselor can read the flip book and discuss the story. Award a band-aid to courageous decision flipbooks. The students can put the band-aid on the flipbook. Students can volunteer to share their stories.

Processing Questions/Conclusion:
Close the session by letting students know that some decisions are not as easy as the ones you asked at the beginning of the session. Some problems require us to make courageous decisions. Sometimes, we may even experience feelings that make us uncomfortable, for example, being scared, etc. But always remember this quote, "If not me, who? If not now, when?"

Cautions:
Be sure to walk around and review the flip book topics as the students are working. Some students may bring up serious issues that may be more appropriately addressed during individual sessions.

Credit/References:
Rangel, B. H., & Norcross, H. (1998). *The band-aid chicken: A program about resisting peer pressure.* Warminster, PA: Marco Products.

About the Group Workers:
Monica Hunter, Ph.D., is a former elementary and secondary School Counselor currently working as a Counselor Educator at the University of South Alabama.

Shanell Petty, M.Ed., is a former School Counselor at the high school level and is currently a School Counselor in a middle school

Activities for Adolescents and Pre-Adolescents

Influences on My Life
Submitted by Jennifer Combs

Session Goals:

- ✓ To identify people in one's life who were influential, either positively or negatively
- ✓ To think about these influences and identify how these influences are manifested in one's behavior
- ✓ To determine how individuals may use this information

Target population: Ages 14-18

Potential Stage/Session(s): Working stage

Estimated Time Length: 45 minutes to 1 hour

Materials: Handout *Influences on My Life*

Activity:
Invite each group member write his/her name in the center circle of the handout. Ask them to think about all of the people (relatives, friends, teachers, coaches, etc.) who have influenced their lives to this point—either in a positive or negative way.

Instruct the students to write the names of these influential people in the circles attached to the "spokes" connecting them to their own circle. On the circumference of each of these circles, have the group write adjectives that describe the person whose name is in each circle.

After all are finished, have each member share his/her own diagram and tell something about each "influence." Encourage each member to consider communicating his/her feelings toward those people identified on the diagram who had positive influences on their lives.

Processing Questions/Conclusion:

- ✓ Was it difficult or easy to come up with your "influences?"
- ✓ How did it feel to write adjectives describing these people?
- ✓ How did it feel to tell the group about your diagram?
- ✓ Do you think you will write to any of your positive "influences?"
- ✓ Was this exercise helpful to you? Why or why not?

Additional Comments:
Depending on your group and its purpose, this activity could be done identifying only positive influences on members' lives.

About the Group Worker:
Jennifer Combs is a graduate student in Mental Health Counseling at Walsh University in North Canton, Ohio.

INFLUENCES ON MY LIFE

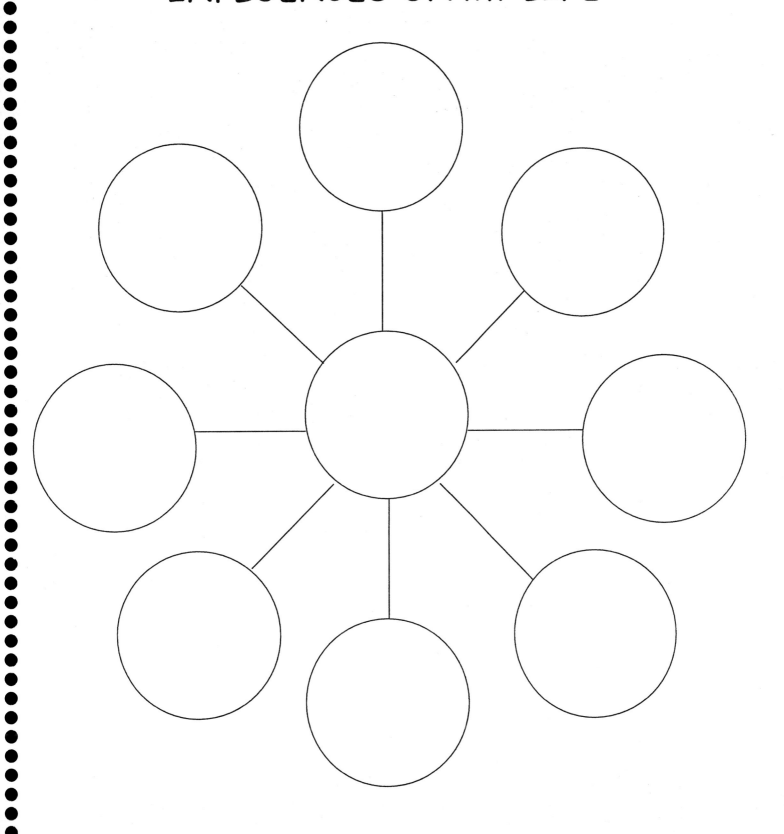

Completing the Puzzle

Submitted by S. Lenoir Gillam

Goals:
- ✓ Help members become better acquainted with one another
- ✓ Reflect on the purpose of the group
- ✓ Understand the difference between individual and group goals
- ✓ Identify assets that each member contributes to the group

Target population: Ages 14-18

Potential Stage/Session(s): Orientation stage/ First session

Estimated Time Length: 25-30 minutes

Materials: Paper (or index cards) and pens or pencils for group members to take notes; puzzle pieces (see *Figure 1*); card stock on which to print or draw puzzle

Note about puzzle shown in *Figure 1*: For six-member groups, this puzzle may be simply enlarged and copied onto card stock. For groups of other sizes, the group leader can create a similar puzzle with the appropriate number of pieces. In either case, the leader needs to have the puzzle pieces cut prior to the group session so that every member can be given one piece.

Activity: Provide each member with: (1) a piece of paper or an index card, (2) a pencil or pen, and (3) one piece of the puzzle.

Specific Directions for Activity:
This is a puzzle activity that will help us explore individual and group goals. Each of you should have a pen (or pencil), an index card (or piece of paper), and one puzzle piece. Please keep your puzzle piece turned upside down until a later point in the activity.

Now, please take a minute and think of a goal you are willing to share with the other members that you hope to achieve during your participation in this group over the next ___ weeks (note to leader: fill in the blank with the number of sessions you have planned for this group). Please record this goal on one side of your index card.

Next, I would like for you to think about one contribution you believe you can make as a member of this group. In other words, what is one of your strengths that you believe will make you an effective group member? For example, you might be a very good listener and think that this quality helps people feel comfortable when communicating with you. On the other side of your index card, please write down the asset you believe you can contribute to this group.

Now that each of you has identified an individual goal you would like to achieve and also a contribution you can make to this group, we will take turns sharing these with the group. You may reference the notes you recorded on your index card. After you mention your group contribution, please place your puzzle piece in the center of the table with the design side showing. (Note to leader: Group member "A" shares the individual goal and then the group contribution and then turns in the puzzle piece before group member "B" takes a turn and so on.) Please wait until everyone has participated before we assemble the puzzle. (Allow members to put together the puzzle.)

Processing Questions/Conclusion:
- ✓ What do you notice about our finished product?
- ✓ What if one member's piece of the puzzle is missing?
- ✓ How does each member's participation contribute to the completion of the puzzle?
- ✓ How are members' individual goals similar?
- ✓ How are members' individual goals different?
- ✓ How can we work together to insure that the group goals are met while also helping members achieve their individual goals?
- ✓ Think of the asset you wrote down as a possible contribution to this group.
- ✓ How will these strengths help the group achieve its goals?
- ✓ How is our group like this puzzle?
- ✓ What does this activity tell us about the importance of group work?

Cautions:
Group ground rules, including confidentiality, must be covered prior to engaging in this activity. In addition, setting up the activity by letting members know that they will be sharing with other members and by communicating the expectation that only one goal and one contribution are being requested is important in minimizing the risk associated with participation. Although the activity is designed to be a low-risk activity and is intended to promote participation, the completion of the task will be impacted by members' willingness to be involved. If a member wishes to "pass" on sharing an individual goal or contribution to the group, then the processing questions may create more challenging dynamics.

Additional Comments:
The activity is appropriate for a variety of groups (e.g., psychoeducational, counseling; see ASGW, 2000) regardless of topic. Based on the logistics of the puzzle assembly and the time needed for everyone to share, the activity is best suited for groups with six or fewer members.

Credit/References:
Association for Specialists in Group Work (ASGW). (2000). ASGW: Professional standards for the training of group workers. *Journal for Specialists in Group Work, 25,* 327-342.

About the Group Worker:
S. Lenoir Gillam, Ph.D., is a Professor in the Department of Counseling, Educational Leadership, and Professional Studies at Columbus State University in Georgia.

Figure 1

Completing the Puzzle Group Activity
S. Lenoir Gillam

Thinking about Self and Career Development
Submitted by Angela D. Coker

Goals:
- ✓ Help group members develop reflection and dialogue about career aspirations
- ✓ Assist group members in getting to know each other
- ✓ Develop cohesion and peer support among group members

Target population: Ages 14-18

Potential Stage/Session(s): Orientation stage/ Initial session ice-breaker activity

Estimated Time Length: Forty-five minutes to one hour

Materials: Name tags, paper and pencil

Introduction to the Activity: Inform group participants that this exercise is designed to help them think about their personal attributes, skills, interests, and career development. It is important to preface this exercise with a discussion about the importance of planning and understanding self before adequately selecting a career or major. In addition, it will be useful to discuss career development within the context of gender. For example, girls have many more career options available to them now as opposed to 50 years ago. Further, for some groups, it may be necessary to discuss the differences between a career versus a job (i.e., A career is something you prepare yourself and requires specialized education and/or technical training such as being a lawyer, doctor, teacher, mechanic, law enforcement officer, etc.).

Activity: Have group participants sit in a circle (preferably in chairs that have built-in desks in front of them). Instruct members to fold their paper into five sections: Each section on the paper will provide space for answers to the following questions: What are my likes and dislikes? What am I good at in terms of my talents and abilities? What subjects do I like in school? What are my career interests and goals for the future? What's one thing I can do to learn more about a particular career or major?

Read aloud each question and ask group members to write their responses in the columns on their papers. You may repeat questions if necessary giving members enough time to respond. After each question has been answered by group participants, invite each to share their responses.

Processing Questions/Conclusion:
Once all members have shared their responses, ask the following questions:
- ✓ What was it like to share your responses with the group?
- ✓ What new things did you learn about yourself and others in the group?
- ✓ Was there something another group member said that sparked your thinking about career planning and development in a different way?
- ✓ What career learning strategies are you most likely to try in the future?

Cautions:
Not all group members will be ready to self-disclose due to shyness or fear of appearing to brag. Further, not every group member will have the same level of awareness or vocabulary regarding personal strengths or career planning. Be sure to encourage their participation and validate their journeys in the discussion.

In terms of multicultural considerations, be sure to honor and respect the diverse backgrounds of all group participants (particularly those who say they have to consult with their parents or other family members before making decisions about career selection). In this case, invite the group participant(s) to think about the career choices they have been discussing with their family members. Invite them to talk more about their skills, personal strengths and strategies for gaining more information about that chosen careers.

Credit/References:
Corey, M. S., & Corey, G. (2006). *Groups: Process and practice (7th ed.).* Belmont, CA: Brooks/Cole.

About the Group Worker:
Angela D. Coker, Ph.D., LPC, NCC, is an Assistant Professor of Counseling and Family Therapy at the University of Missouri – St. Louis.

Look at Me in a Sugar Cookie
Submitted by Stephanie Markey

Goals:
- ✓ To discuss what each member has learned about him/herself though the group process
- ✓ To share how they have changed through the process
- ✓ To share their thoughts with other members on how each have changed or grown

Target population: Ages 10 and up

Potential Stage/Session: Termination

Estimated Time: 45 minutes

Materials:
- ✓ Large round sugar cookies – one for each group member
- ✓ Plastic knives
- ✓ Icing in a variety of colors and flavors
- ✓ Food coloring, icing "pens"
- ✓ Sprinkle toppings
- ✓ Napkins and paper plates

Activity: Give each member one cookies, a plate, a plastic knife, and a napkin. Have the different candies, sprinkles, icings, etc. set up on a long table. Instruct members to sit alone and, without talking to others, design a cookie that reflects something about themselves, what they know about themselves, how they have changed or grown through the group process. When everyone is finished, each will share the symbolism of their own cookies with the group.

Processing Questions/Conclusion:

- ✓ What is the purpose of this activity?
- ✓ How did it feel to design a cookie that represents you?
- ✓ What comments do you have for your group members?
- ✓ Were you surprised by any of the cookies?
- ✓ Can you see how easy it is to show who we are in something as simple as a cookie?
- ✓ What might this have been like if we did the activity at the very beginning of the group?
- ✓ Enjoy your cookie!

About the Group Worker:
Stephanie Markey, M.A., PCC, is a stay-at-home mother who has worked as a mental health counselor in the Youngstown City Schools, Youngstown, Ohio.

Good Credit, Bad Debt
Submitted by David Hermon and Terri McConda

Goals:
- ✓ Assist student in understanding credit and credit cards
- ✓ Differentiate between good debt and bad debt

Target population: Ages 14-18
Ideal for students preparing for greater independence in financial areas of their lives.

Potential Stage/Session: Orientation stage/ Second or third session of a college admissions counseling group

Estimated Time Length: 25 minutes

Materials: Paper and pencil; Interest rate tables

Activity: As an introductory activity on how compound interest works, ask students if they would rather (1) get paid ten thousand dollars per month, or (2) earn 1 penny on the first day of each month that doubles every day ($0.01 first day, $0.02 second day, $0.04 third day, $0.08 fourth day, etc.). Visit the web page for an exercise that shows a table for how much they would have at the end of each month: *http://www.elevateurbanyouth.org/v2/new/Grades1-4/SavingsInterest1-4.htm* (Note: On day thirty of each month they would earn $5,368,709.12 if they chose option 2).

Then ask students what percent interest they believe they earn on money they put into a saving vehicle (bank savings account, on-line money market, etc.). Present a table showing interest compounding for ten years at 3%.

Have students describe the benefits of having a credit card (ease of use, flexibility, safer than carrying cash, etc.). Ask the students what percent of interest they believe the pay on money spent? Present a table showing interest compounding for ten years at 18%.

Ask whether all debt bad debt? Can you always afford to pay in cash? (For dinner with friends, a movie, or a car, college tuition, a home, etc.)
"Rules of thumb" on debt:
- ✓ Never go in debt for a depreciating asset.
- ✓ A home is something that you believe will appreciate in value.
- ✓ A college education is an investment in the most important thing – you!
- ✓ Debt that a person accrues to live a lifestyle beyond your means is not investing in you. In fact, it is robbing you of future opportunities such as the opportunity to live where you would like to live, to donate to causes, to educate in new ways, etc.
- ✓ Keeping up with the Jones' is a recipe for disaster.

College loans:
- ✓ Investing in yourself for college assuming you have a realistic grasp on what you would like to study is one of the best investments you can make.
- ✓ Financial experts recently reported at a 2007 Senator Edward M. Kennedy committee meeting on college affordability that financial aid debt for graduating college students has risen to an average of $17,500.
- ✓ Explain the differences between federal and private loans.

The Importance of Good Credit:
- ✓ Discuss the benefits of establishing credit (credit card, installment loan, etc.) and building a good credit history. When the time comes to apply for a mortgage, you'll want to have a good *credit score (FICO)* in order to get the loan at a good interest rate.

Explain the FICO score and the 3 Cs:
- ✓ <u>Character</u> can be judged by reviewing a loan applicant's credit history: bills paid on time, loans paid back, etc.
- ✓ <u>Capacity</u> is the ability of the borrower to make payments on the loan. It is determined by looking at the borrower's current and future earnings.
- ✓ <u>Collateral</u> means assets like cars, houses, stocks, and bonds; i.e., things the borrower could sell in order to pay off a loan.

Processing Questions/Conclusion:
Choose among the following areas to continue a discussion based on the needs / priorities of the group:
- ✓ Paying yourself first
- ✓ Staying out of debt
- ✓ Living within your means
- ✓ How bad financial choices impact your life
- ✓ How this information be useful to you in the future

Credit/References:
Dunbar, D. (2007). *What you don't know can keep you out of college.* New York: Gotham Books.
http://kennedy.senate.gov/newsroom/press_release.cfm?id=6D1846F5-6AA4-4A9E-8F7D-7A0C5D556BEC

About the Group Workers:
David A. Hermon, Ph.D., is a Professor of Counseling at Marshall University.

Terri McConda, M.A., is a School Counselor and teacher at Russell High School in Ashland Kentucky.

Handling Feelings about Deployment

Submitted by Melanie Korth, Pit Kolodinsky, and Cristina Gonzales

Goals:
- ✓ To share similar feelings of anxiety, fear, separation and loss with other students whose parents or other family members are deployed.
- ✓ To learn coping skills by sharing with others how their family roles changed during deployment and how they were able to have their needs met when their parents were apart during separation, as well as when they were together during reunion.
- ✓ To help children of deployed parents be better able to concentrate and be more productive at school.

Target population: Ages 12-18; Students who have a family member that is deployed, recently returned or expecting to be deployed. Can be adapted for younger children.

Potential Stage/Session(s): Orientation stage/First and second sessions, continuing depending on students' needs

Estimated Time Length: 45 minutes each session, once a week while family member is deployed as well as during re-entry process

Materials: Art materials for students to express how they feel, to make posters and to decorate the bulletin board. We used colored construction paper, scissors, glue, poster board, glitter, colored markers, colored pencils, crayons, paper, envelopes and stamps.

Activity: Group discussion is the primary technique used where each student is given the opportunity to speak. Members are encouraged to listen respectfully to what other students are saying and are expected to share and support other members.

Session 1
- ✓ Discuss the purpose and rules of the group and review confidentiality.
- ✓ Members introduce themselves.
- ✓ Member's family constellation is discussed and each member is encouraged to describe their family and the parent or family member that is deployed.
- ✓ Group members may self-disclose about their relationships with the deployed parent or family member and how they feel about the separation.
- ✓ If a student's parent or family member returns home, the student should have the opportunity to express the emotions he or she experienced.
- ✓ The goal is for them to feel that they are not alone in their situation and create a climate of trust.

Session 2

✓ In order to help with effective coping mechanisms during deployment, group members would be asked to describe a situation that was difficult to handle with their mom, dad, brother or sister gone. They could brainstorm ways to handle the situation more effectively next time.

✓ Acknowledge that the remaining parent and other family members are also affected by the separation.

✓ Members discuss how their roles have changed since their parent was deployed.

✓ Members discuss their feelings about the group and what they have learned.

✓ Students find support knowing that other students are experiencing what they are going through and when these students have been identified, they may provide support to each other in school or out.

Processing Questions/Conclusion:

✓ Have students email or write letters to their absent parent or family member.

✓ Have students draw a picture of themselves with their family.

✓ Have students draw posters to hang around school: "Support our troops! Wear red on Fridays."

✓ Have group members decorate a "hero" bulletin board with photos and a star representing each deployed parent.

Cautions:

Military deployment, with thousands of our troops being separated from their families for long periods of time, has a profound impact on family members left behind. It is important to be sensitive to the anxiety, grief and fear these students experience.

Credit/References:

Corey, M.S., & Corey G. (2006). *Groups: Process and practice.* Belmont, CA: Thompson Brooks/Cole.

Hardy, L. (2006, December). When kids lose parents in our war in Iraq. *Education Digest, 72(4),* 10-12.

Mitchum, N.T. (1991, May). Group counseling for Navy children. *School Counselor, 38(5),* 372-377.

Mitchum, N.T. (1999, September). The effects of group counseling on the self-esteem, anxiety and behavior of children with deployed parents. *Dissertation Abstracts International: The Sciences and Engineering,* 60(3B), 1309.

Swartz, M. (2006, March). Heartbreak high. *Texas Monthly, 34(3),* 150-272.

About the Group Workers:

Melanie Korth, a retired Marine Corps Major, is a School Counseling graduate student at Northern Arizona University, Yuma Campus.

Pit Kolodinsky, Ph.D., is an Associate Professor of Counseling at Northern Arizona University.

Cristina Gonzales is currently a School Counseling graduate student at Northern Arizona University, Yuma Campus.

A Better Alternative
Submitted by Marian Beresh

Goals:
- ✓ To raise students awareness of the consequences of using alcohol or other drugs
- ✓ To consider possible ways to replace those behaviors.

Target Population: Ages 14-18

Potential Stage/Session: Working

Estimated Time Length: 45 minutes

Materials: Worksheets #1 and #2, pens or pencils for each member

Activity:

      Students who have used substances are given this activity to begin to think beyond the "buzz." Students are given the Activity Sheet #1 to begin processing possible consequences of drug/alcohol use, both short and long term. Group members will then process their answers with the group. The group leader then raises the possibility of replacing the substance use behavior with appropriate ways to spend one's time. Students are also encouraged to think about their life goals. Worksheet #2 is distributed, completed, and then processed. Discussion is led to help the students tie their current behaviors to the consequences and to explore ways to replace the substance use behaviors with more positive acceptable ones.

      The activity could be concluded with students sharing their plans for that day or weekend to help them start planning activities ahead of time in order to have a plan for their "free time."

Processing Questions/Conclusion:
- ✓ How can your behaviors be replaced?
- ✓ Is it difficult for you to stop using?
- ✓ Do you need help to reach your goals?
- ✓ Who can help you?
- ✓ How do you feel about doing the alternative activities you have listed?
- ✓ Will you actually do these other activities?

Additional Comments:

It is helpful to check in with students intermittently outside of group and check on the progress/status of the replacement behaviors.

About the Group Worker:

Marian Beresh, M.A., PC, is a Ph.D. candidate in Counselor Education and Supervision at Kent State University, in Kent, Ohio and a current School Counselor at Jackson High School in Massillon, Ohio.

A Better Alternative
Worksheet #1

What I can do to stop using: _____
(drug used to lead me to this group)

Consequences at school:

```
┌─────────────────────────────────────────────────────────┐
│                                                           │
│                                                           │
│                                                           │
│                                                           │
│                                                           │
└─────────────────────────────────────────────────────────┘
```

Consequences at home/family:

```
┌─────────────────────────────────────────────────────────┐
│                                                           │
│                                                           │
│                                                           │
│                                                           │
└─────────────────────────────────────────────────────────┘
```

If I continue, possible consequences as an adult:

```
┌─────────────────────────────────────────────────────────┐
│ (Career)                                                  │
│                                                           │
│ (Law)                                                     │
│                                                           │
│ (Relationships)                                           │
│                                                           │
│ (Money)                                                   │
│                                                           │
│ Other:                                                    │
│                                                           │
└─────────────────────────────────────────────────────────┘
```

A Better Alternative
Worksheet #2

Other things to do instead of using: _____
                                       (drug used to lead me to this group)

At school I can:

After school or on the weekends I can:

If I stop using now I have a better chance of reaching my own goals in life:

1._____

2._____

3._____

4._____

5._____

Career Options: Exploring Self-Truths

Submitted by Natalie Kosine and Sandra Duncan

Goals:
- ✓ Develop a deeper sense of self-awareness about career desires and the role that personality plays in long-term career satisfaction
- ✓ Develop a purpose-centered perspective regarding career exploration and decision-making
- ✓ Understand the importance of being knowledgeable and proactive in career decision-making
- ✓ Become aware of the education and/or training required to achieve career goals

Target population: Ages 14-18

Potential Stage/Session(s): Orientation stage/ Initial sessions of career exploration group

Estimated Time Length: 45 minutes to one hour

Materials: Paper and pencil to complete a journal activity.
Additionally, each member will need to complete the Strong Interest Inventory (or a comparable career assessment) prior to the first group session where results of the assessment will be made available.

Activity: Following an introduction by the facilitator as to the purpose of the group, members are asked to write down three major characteristics of their personality and share with the group. The leader then facilitates a discussion about the importance of knowing oneself in relation to career (e.g., work environment preferences, activity preferences, etc.), in addition to the question: What does it mean to "know thyself?" The facilitator explains that knowing oneself consists of knowing one's beliefs, desires, identity, and personality traits and requires that we engage in introspection. Further, the group discusses the ways in which self-knowledge is an important part of career exploration and career choice.

The group then reviews their SII results. The facilitator helps the participants navigate and interpret their results. The participants break into small groups of 2-3 to discuss the following: In what way do the results of the SII fit me or not fit me? What is most surprising? What career(s) seem interesting? Of the SII career suggestions, which one's look meaningful and how? How can I use this information in my career decision-making?

Processing Questions/Conclusion:
Self-Truths: Next, the group members, using their SII as a guide, write down three to five truths about themselves in relation to career and interests using the lead-in terms (e.g., I am, I like, I want, I can, I'm interested, I don't like, etc.) and share their responses with the group. Using the results of their SII and their journal responses, the participants are asked to write down three to five careers that they find interesting, that fit their personality characteristics, and that compliment their self-truths. Participants share their responses with the group.

Additional Comments:
To adequately cover all of the material above, you may want to split this into two group sessions.

About the Group Workers:
Natalie Kosine, Ph.D., is Assistant Professor of Educational and Counseling Psychology at the University of Louisville.

Sandra Duncan, Ph.D., is an Assistant Professor of Educational and Counseling Psychology at the University of Louisville.

Risk Bag
Submitted by Jon M. Coventry

Session Goals: To help introduce group members to each other and to assist the members to feel comfortable in the group setting and with each other and the group leader(s). To encourage the group members to move forward in their treatment by taking risks and sharing at a deeper level with each other.

Target population: Ages 14-18

Potential Stage/Session(s): Transition stage

Estimated Time Length: 45 minutes to one hour

Materials: Brown paper lunch bag marked "Risk Bag." Sentence stems copied on paper and cut into strips with one sentence stem on each piece of paper. All or some of the sentence stems (see below) may be used.

Activity:
This activity uses a brown paper bag filled with various sentence stems to help deepen group member relationships and general group cohesion.

Specific Directions for Activity:
Place sentence stems in the brown lunch bag marked "Risk Bag." Briefly make a presentation about risk taking. Point out that each participant may choose his/her own level of risk when completing the sentence he/she draws from the bag.

A volunteer reaches into the bag and selects one strip. Group member reads the sentence stem to the group and then completes however he/she wishes. Others may comment or question the response, keeping group norms in mind. The bag is then passed to the next group member and that member chooses, reads and completes the sentence stem. The bag goes around the group circle and all members participate including the group facilitator(s). The number of sentence stems that each participant answers depends on how much time the activity has been allotted as a part of the group for this session. This activity tends to lead into more serious group discussions depending on the nature of the statements made by each group member.

Processing Questions/Conclusion:
 Process with the group members how they felt about sharing some previously unknown details about themselves and their lives with each other.

- ✓ On a scale of 1-10, how difficult was this activity (with 1 being most easy and 10 being most difficult)?
- ✓ What were you most surprised about?
- ✓ Taking positive risks can be scary at times, but personal growth often depends on doing things and saying things that we are not always comfortable with. Do you feel different after sharing (or hearing) particular information about yourself or others? Why or why not?
- ✓ Whose courage in sharing was most impressive to you today?

Conclude by affirming and thanking participants for taking risks and sharing who they are with the rest of the group.

Cautions:
Some group members may not be ready to share about themselves with the rest of the group even though most of the sentence stems are non-threatening and could actually serve as ice-breakers. Members could be given the option of passing if there is a sentence stem they choose not to respond to. Facilitator(s) should determine ahead of time if passing is an option and how many times the group members are permitted to skip their turn. Also, depending on the educational level of the group members, the group leader(s) should be sensitive to the fact that there may be group members who are not comfortable reading the sentence stems aloud or who may not have the ability to read.

Additional Comments:
The sentence stems can be adapted and varied to fit the population of the group, including children, adolescents and adults.

About the Group Worker:
Jon M. Coventry, M.A., PCC-s, is a school-based clinical counselor currently working in elementary and middle schools in Stark County, Ohio.

Risk Bag Sentence Stems

I am most happy when...

An important goal for me is...

Sometimes I worry about...

When I was young, I...

When someone ignores me, I...

I am looking forward to...

I wish I could change...

Today my body feels...

It makes me sad when...

If I could change one thing about myself, I would...

I want others to know that I...

I get annoyed whenever...

The thought of getting old makes me...

Something that I really like about myself is...

A law I would like to see enforced is...

Something no one knows about me is...

I would have more peace of mind if...

When under a lot of stress, I...

When someone criticizes me, I...

When I feel depressed, I...

My feelings were hurt when...

If I needed to be comforted, I would turn to...

I feel most relaxed and peaceful when...

When I think of the future, I...

I cry when...

The thing that scares me the most is...

Most people don't know that I...

I dream about...

Something I want to see before I die is...

I wonder if...

If I could relive one year of my life, it would be...

When I am alone, I...

I feel happy and content when...

My idea of a good day or evening is...

I am so thankful for...

Someone I really admire is... because...

If I had an emergency at 4:00am, I would call...

Something I will never do is...

I once felt guilty about...

Most of the time, I feel... about myself.

Something I feel I need to do is...

Two things I want to accomplish in my life are...

When I feel embarrassed, I...

My perfect world would be...

Something I believe about love is...

When I think of my childhood, I...

The person who has most influenced my life is...

Something interesting I have learned about life is...

Colors of Memories (Negative)

Submitted by Bengu Erguner-Tekinalp

Goals:
- ✓ Share unpleasant childhood memories
- ✓ Talk about negative memories and how they affect current experiences
- ✓ Develop an awareness of how memories of the past effect us today

Target population: Ages 13-18

Potential Stage/Session(s): Working stage

Estimated Time Length: 40-50 minutes

Materials: None

Activity: Ask the participants to think back to their childhood before middle school and recall an unpleasant memory. Ask them to think about the experience and stay with the feeling. Ask the participants to pick a color that describes the feeling. Then, have participants pair up and talk about the color they picked for the experience. When everyone has shared with each other let them come in to the big group and ask volunteers to talk about the colors chosen.

Processing Questions/Conclusion:
- ✓ How easy/difficult was it to remember an unhappy time?
- ✓ How easy/difficult was it to stay with the feeling?
- ✓ How did it feel to describe and share experience as a color to your partner?
- ✓ Do you think this experience has an effect on your life today? If so in what ways?
- ✓ Why do you think you remembered this event?

Cautions:
The group worker needs to be careful as some students may have difficulty remembering a very negative experience from their childhood.

Additional Comments:
This activity can be used by just sharing the experiences with each other without picking a color that represents the experience

About the Group Worker:
Bengu Erguner-Tekinalp, Ph.D., is a Counselor Educator at the Drake University, Iowa.

Colors of Memories (Positive)
Submitted by Bengu Erguner-Tekinalp

Goals:
✓ Share joyful childhood memories
✓ Talk about happy memories and how they affect current experiences
✓ Develop an awareness of how memories of the past effect us today

Target population: Ages 13-18

Potential Stage/Session(s): Working stage

Estimated Time Length: 40-50 minutes

Materials: None

Activity:
Ask the participants to think back to their childhood before middle school and remember an experience they recall with absolute happiness and joy. Ask them to think about the experience and stay with the feeling. Ask the participants to pick a color that describes the feeling. Then, have participants pair up and talk about the color they picked for the experience. When everyone has shared with each other let them come in to the big group and ask volunteers to talk about the colors chosen.

Processing Questions/Conclusion:
✓ How easy/difficult was it to remember a time of joy and happiness?
✓ How easy/difficult was it to stay with the feeling?
✓ How did it feel to describe and share experience as a color to your partner?
✓ Do you think this experience has an effect on your life today? If so in what ways?
✓ Why do you think you remembered this event?

Cautions:
The group worker needs to be careful as some students may have difficulty remembering a very positive experience from their childhood.

Additional Comments:
This activity can be used by just sharing the experiences with each other without picking a color that represents the experience

About the Group Worker:
Bengu Erguner-Tekinalp, Ph.D., is a Counselor Educator at the Drake University, Iowa.

The Computer Game

Submitted by George R. Leddick

Goals:
- ✓ Assist students in getting acquainted
- ✓ Develop listening skills

Target population: Ages 11-18

Potential Stage/Session(s): Orientation stage/ First, second, or third sessions

Estimated Time Length: 30 minutes for 20 students (Duration may be modified)

Materials: Sufficient space for movement, a list of questions

Activity: This get acquainted activity focuses on movement and energy. On the safe versus challenging continuum, it does not require much in terms of self disclosure.

The key to this exercise is issuing instructions that are brief and concise. Give participants the first instruction; once they have complied give them the second instruction. Do not give instructions all at once.

Specific Directions for Activity:
Today we will play a game called "The Computer Game." First, we need two teams. Each team will be a computer. When I point to you say either "1" or "2." Now all the "number 1's line up here. Number 2's line up here. (There should be two parallel lines, facing each other, with sufficient room for you to walk between the rows. When assigning numbers, I try to split talkative versus quiet people evenly).

Now you are part of a computer. This row is one computer, and this other row is another computer. Each person is one chip; a computer memory chip. As a memory chip, you only know your own information. You can only SPEAK your own information. I repeat, the only words you can say, as a computer chip, are your one answer—except for that, chips can't talk.

So here's how we play. When I ask the computer something, the computer sorts it. So if I say, "Computer, tell me first names!" It is your job to do two things. You say your own first name over and over so the rest of your team can hear. Then you sort into alphabetical order. You have to hear what the other chips are saying in order to stand in the right place.

Let's try a practice run. This one doesn't count. I will stand at this end of both computers. The people closest to me will be closest to "A" in the alphabet, and a "Z" would be farthest away in line. Let's see which computer can sort the fastest, while you can only say your answer. (Modeling) If I wanted to find my place in line, I would say "George, George, George, George...." and at the same time listen to my teammates tell me their names. When I think I am in the right spot I get in line and keep saying my name "George, George..." to help the other chips in my computer find their spot.

So let's try that now: Computer, tell me first names.
(Remind chips they are only allowed to say their own name).

Okay! That was fun! This computer finished first, and therefore they were faster this time. But we also have to see if this computer was both FAST and ACCURATE. So we will have the other computer "verify" their answers to be sure they are in the right order. So when I point to you, say your answer. (Repeat each child's answer so all can hear.)

Okay, other computer, were they right? Was anyone out of order? (If anyone was found to be out of alphabetical order and/or simply changed locations once realizing it, this means the computer finished moving AFTER the other computer and the second computer wins....IF they were also accurate.)

Let's see if the second computer was accurate. You know what they say about "Slow but sure." They might be dependable! Say your answer when I point at you. (Repeat each name so all can hear). Okay, other computer, were they all in the correct position?

Now you know how to play. You repeat your information out loud, then you sort yourself. Letter As are closer to me. If the answer is a number, the 1s are closer to me.

Let's try another: Computer, tell me LAST names.

Once sorted, have both computers check each other for accuracy by repeating each answer.

Other sample questions:
- ✓ Computer, tell me your favorite color.
- ✓ Computer, what would you buy first if you won the $200 million lottery?
- ✓ Computer, what was the name of your all time favorite pet?
- ✓ Computer, name your favorite Musician (alternates: movie, book, team, hobby)
- ✓ Computer, what's the NAME of the city/town that's farthest from here—where YOU have been? NAME the farthest you've been. (Confirm this is alphabetical by name, not numerical by miles)

Number questions:
- ✓ Computer, how many people live in your house ? (Remember, Ones are closest to me)
- ✓ Computer, how many people who live in your home are older than you?
- ✓ Computer, how many people who live in your home are younger than you?
- ✓ Computer, how many schools have you been to?
- ✓ Computer, how many towns have you lived in (ever!).
- ✓ Computer how many groups have you been in before?

The sample questions above are for illustration purposes and your substitutions can be tailor made to reflect the interests of this age/maturity level. Begin with simple questions that require little disclosure. Make questions concise, age appropriate and relevant to the people involved. Some of the last questions might include the purpose of this particular group: (e.g.: A Loss Group--How many pets have you had that died? How many people have you ever known, who have died?)

Through practice you will learn how to guess the length of time the activity will keep this particular group engaged. When guessing, err on the side of leaving them wanting more. You will always need a few easy warm up questions, and you will always wish to ask questions later that are pertinent to the group's topic. You will thus ask more or fewer intermediate questions, depending upon attention span. Remember you will be monitoring each set of answers for accuracy and repeating each answer for every person so the group hears all information.

Processing Questions/Conclusion:

- ✓ Whew ! Are you tired from all that sorting and thinking? What was that game like for you?
- ✓ What did you learn about our whole group ? For example, I noticed lots of us have short last names. What did you notice ? (Retain focus on group as a whole). There will be several themes to notice: e.g. large versus small families, not many had pets, few world travelers, a variety of musical tastes, ...EVERYONE has someone in their family who died. (OK, so that wasn't accidental, they were screened, but now they know too)
- ✓ Were any of you SURPRISED by any characteristic of our group?
- ✓ Did this game help us get to know individuals better, or did we profile the whole group? Which was easier for you to see? (Unlike many get acquainted activities, this exercise is better at profiling the whole group—and serving as an energizer.)
- ✓ Optional : Did anyone here INTEND to hurt anyone else's feelings with their answer? No ? OK. Did anyone get their feelings hurt inadvertently? No? OK. One rule for our group is: Nobody is allowed to hurt anyone else on purpose. Agreed?

Cautions:
Consider whether or not every student is physically able to participate. Remember that children already excited do not require energizers, so late Friday afternoons would probably be avoided. When participants begin to give alphabetical answers so they can stay in one spot, it is time to switch to number answers or perhaps time to end.

Credit/References:
Pfeiffer, J.W., & Jones, J.E. (Eds.) (1993). *The annual handbook for group facilitators.* San Diego: University Associates.

About the Group Worker:
Dr. George R. Leddick is a Counselor Educator, a former ASGW Past-President, and a Fellow of the Association for Specialists in Group Work (ASGW).

Props in a Box
Submitted by Melissa Luke

Goals:
- ✓ Assist students in articulating their individual needs and hopes for group behavior
- ✓ Move toward agreement on a set of shared ground rules (The 'props in a box' remain present for all future group sessions and can be referred to as necessary)

Target Population: Ages 11-18
This group may also be used with 4th and 5th grade groups capable of abstract thinking.

Potential Stage/Session(s): Orientation stage/First or second sessions of group

Estimated Time Length: Approximately 30-40 minutes

Materials:
In addition to a small size toolbox, the activity requires a minimum of 30-40 'props.' These props can be small toys, household items, random found objects, and actual tools.

Some possible examples include the following: keys, large paperclip, bottle cap, human figures, pinecone, credit card, play dishes, bar of soap, roll of masking tape, match box car, wrench, floppy disc, bird nest, envelope, plastic animals, sea shell, and eraser.

Activity:
A toolbox and props are used to assist students in developing rules for the group. The props may then be used over the course of the group to reinforce maintenance of group rules.

Specific Directions for Activity:
Before beginning the activity itself, the counselor introduces the idea of symbolic expression/ physical metaphor. Depending upon the age of the students involved, the counselor tailors the definition accordingly.

Examples can also be useful, with students easily understanding how a brand logo stands for a company, but can also come to represent something else (e.g., Nike swish, Timberland tree, Geico lizard). It is recommended that the counselor has a couple props on hand that will not included in the toolbox itself, so that s/he can use them to demonstrate the activity. For example, a light bulb is often associated with an idea, so in this instance a light bulb might symbolize the expectation that all group members will share their ideas and reactions within the group. Another example could be a padlock that might symbolically express the expectation that group members will guard or lock the confidentiality of what is said in group.

The counselor places the toolbox (full of props), on the floor or a table in the center of the group, with students seated in a surrounding circle. The counselor explains how the activity is an opportunity for all group members to be involved in developing a set of ground rules. Further, the counselor offers that students will use symbolic expression and/or physical metaphor to show and tell what kinds of behaviors they think will/can assist successful participation in the group.

After opening the toolbox and revealing the props inside, the counselor directs each student to select an object that can symbolize a behavior that the student wants to see in the group. When each student has selected an object, each student is invited to do the following:

- ✓ Tell what they selected by naming the prop
- ✓ Explain the expectation for group behavior symbolized by the prop
- ✓ Place the object in the toolbox

After a student places the object in the toolbox, the counselor processes other group members' reactions about the expectation and how it might impact group participation.

When all members have discussed their props and placed them in the toolbox, the counselor asks if there are any props/expectations that the members do not want as ground rules or if there are any additional ones that seem necessary, but have not been mentioned. At this point, the counselor might want to offer ideas and reactions of his or her own. Once agreement is reached, the toolbox is closed and the remaining props are removed from the floor or table. In the remaining time, group members share their experiences of their participation in the activity.

As with all activities, some students engage more readily, while other can struggle with doing so. The counselor may need to encourage, coach, and/or assist some students in their selection of a prop, and with the articulation of the symbolism involved. While it is important for all group members to participate and contribute at least one 'prop' as an expectation for group behavior, the activity itself offers a flexible range of how this can occur.

Processing Questions/Conclusion:

Potential questions that can be used within the activity, as well as after, to process are as follows:

- ✓ What was it about that object that appealed to you?
- ✓ How would it 'look' if this expectation for group behavior was taking place? How would it 'look' if it were not?
- ✓ What do you notice in yourself and other group members right now?
- ✓ Are you aware of any reactions as you're hearing about group members' ideas?
- ✓ What will we do as a group if/when an expectation is not adhered to?
- ✓ How might this expectation help you as an individual group member? How about us a group? What are the differences and how will we negotiate these?
- ✓ What did you like/ dislike about this activity?

✓ How did the use of symbolic expression/ physical metaphor impact your participation today?
✓ What did you learn about yourself, your group members, and the counselor through this activity?

Additional Comments:
The counselor should carefully balance the amount of structure imposed within this activity with the processing that occurs. It is important for the counselor to continually and fluidly monitor and move between the activity itself, the symbolic expression, and the immediate reactions and dynamics within the group.

About the Group Worker:
Melissa Luke, Ph.D., LMHC, NCC, is a former School Counselor and currently works as an Assistant Professor and Coordinator of School Counseling in the Counseling and Human Services department at Syracuse University.

Who am I? Images of My Biracial/Multiracial Self

Submitted by Carmen F. Salazar

Goals:
- ✓ Explore self-concept and physical appearance
- ✓ Gain insight into racial/cultural identity
- ✓ Understand others' perceptions of oneself
- ✓ Receive confirmation and assurance of personal worth

Target population: Ages 11-18; Boys and girls of mixed race heritage.

Potential Stage/Session(s): Orientation stage, revisited and expanded upon during the transition or working stage

Estimated Time Length: 40-50 minutes or longer, depending on number of process questions used, and size and maturity level of group.

Materials: butcher paper, crayons, markers, magazine clippings for collage, a list of "self talk" and messages about self, envelopes to store clippings, glue sticks

Activity:
Along with the developmental challenges associated with adolescence, mixed heritage youth encounter the additional challenge of forging an identity in a society that presses them to choose a monoracial/cultural existence and disavow part of their heritage. They are especially vulnerable to differential treatment by parents and relatives, social rejection by peers, and ambivalent attention in their schools and communities. Research and clinical practice indicates a positive relationship between racial/ethnic identity and self-esteem for mixed heritage children and adolescents.

This activity takes some preplanning. *In an earlier session*, have each group member brainstorm and make a "message list" of self talk and things others say to them about themselves. Relate the message list to their racial/ethnic self. Put the list away to use in this exercise. In addition, prepare for this exercise *the week before* by distributing a variety of magazines to the group members to take home and look through. Ask them to come prepared with images cut or torn from the magazines that "say" something about how they view themselves or others view them. Give each group member an envelope to store the clippings. Also give each group member his or her "message list" to put in the envelope.

Group members will pair up and help each other draw an outline of their body on a piece of butcher paper. Each group member will fill in the outline of him or herself with a collage of clippings, drawings and words (e.g., self talk, messages from others). The collage may be used as a one-time creation or as a work-in-progress to be used in multiple sessions. Group members will take turns sharing their completed drawing. Use the "self-concept and appearance" questions to focus discussion.

Specific Directions for Activity:

Today you're making a "collage" that will help us know *you* and understand some of your thoughts and feelings about being a person of mixed heritage. A "collage" is simply a collection of pictures and words that represent you. This isn't an art project, so you don't have to worry about making a perfect drawing. Once you've finished your collage, everyone will have a chance to tell us about their collage.

I'm going to give each of you a big piece of paper that's as long as you are tall. Pair up with another group member. Take turns lying on your piece of paper, while the other person draws the outline of your body. Watch how I do it. Who will be my helper?

Then take the outline of your body and fill it in. You can glue on the magazine clippings you've stored in the envelope I gave you last week; you can draw pictures, and write in messages (like things you say to yourself about you, or things others say about you).

Processing Questions/Conclusion:

Choose from the following list of "self-concept and appearance" questions, as time allows:

Self-Concept and Appearance:

- ✓ *Who* do you see when you look in the mirror?
- ✓ *What* do you see when you look in the mirror?
- ✓ What do you like the most about what you see?
- ✓ What do you like the least?
- ✓ What do you tell yourself about your appearance?
- ✓ What positive messages do you tell yourself?
- ✓ What negative messages do you tell yourself?

- ✓ What do you hear from *others* (e.g., parents, family, friends, or teachers) about how you look?

- ✓ What does this say about how *they* see your racial self?
- ✓ How does this fit with how *you* see *yourself*?

- ✓ What do you like the *most* about being a person of mixed heritage?
- ✓ What do you like the *least* about it?

Follow-up questions - After each group member has the opportunity to respond to the above questions, ask the following:

- ✓ What did you learn about yourself?
- ✓ What did you learn about others in the group?
- ✓ What similarities and differences did you see in how group members answered?
- ✓ What surprised you the most, and why?

The collage can be used as a "work-in-progress" for use in multiple sessions. In subsequent sessions, group members can be asked to look over their drawings, add or remove clippings, revise the drawing, and add or mark out "self talk" or messages heard from others. Check in with them on what has changed, what has remained the same, and what has affected their choices. Follow up with focused discussion.

The following questions are examples of how group discussion could be focused in subsequent sessions. Vary the choice of questions and wording of the questions based on earlier discussions and on maturity level of the group. Use the same follow-up questions listed above to "wrap up" the session.

Self-Identity and Others' Perceptions:

When filling out forms for school, you (or your parents) are asked to identify your race. Usually, you have to pick *one* box to check (e.g., Black or African American, Caucasian, Hispanic, Native American). On some forms, there are boxes for different races and there's also a box for "Other."
  ✓ If you filled out one of these forms, which box would you check?
  ✓ How easy or difficult is it for you to choose which box?
  ✓ If you could pick more than one box, which ones would you check?
  ✓ How do you/would you feel about checking the box for "Other"?
  ✓ Do you ever feel like an "Other"? What does being an "Other" feel like?

Oftentimes, people of mixed heritage get asked the question: "What are you?"
  ✓ Does that ever happen to you?
  ✓ When people ask you that question how do you feel?
  ✓ What do you think they're really asking?
  ✓ How do you answer?
  ✓ Have you always answered this way? If not, how has your answer changed?
  ✓ What/who helped you figure out how to answer this question?
  ✓ Are there other ways you wish you could answer?

People of mixed heritage come up with different ways to describe their racial selves. Some choose one race, usually the race of one of their parents (e.g., "I'm Black" or "I'm White"). Some include the race of both parents (e.g., "I'm Black *and* White" or "I'm Black *and* Asian *and* White"). Others choose words like *biracial* or *multiracial, biethnic* or *multiethnic.* Some say "I'm mixed." Still others make up a name to describe all the races in their heritage. For example, Tiger Woods is often referred to as African American, but he made up the term *Cablinasian* to describe himself, because he is a racial mixture of Caucasian, Black, Indian, and Asian ancestry.

  ✓ Have you thought about how you would describe yourself?
  ✓ If you have, what words have you thought about that would best describe yourself?
  ✓ How did you come up with this description? What helped you choose?
  ✓ How close does your answer fit with how you see yourself?
  ✓ How does your answer fit with how you look?
  ✓ How does your answer fit with how you think others see you?
  ✓ If you have brothers or sisters, how similar or different is your answer from theirs?

116

What assumptions do others make about you based on your appearance?
What assumptions do others make about you based on what they know about your parents' racial heritage?

Peer Relationships and Dating:

In some schools, when kids sit in the cafeteria all the White kids sit together, all the Black kids sit together, all the Latino/Hispanic kids sit together, and all the Asian kids or the Native American kids sit together, and sometimes there are mixed tables, and so on.

- ✓ Who do you sit with?
- ✓ Who would you like to sit with?
- ✓ How do you decide? Is it your choice or is the choice made for you?
- ✓ How do these choices affect who you'll be friends with at school?
- ✓ How do these choices affect who you go out with?

Cautions:
Some students may have limited access to magazines. Build a collection of magazines ahead of time and distribute to the group members to take home and look through to prepare for the activity.

Credit/References:
I first learned of the "draw and fill in the outline of your body" activity during my master's internship at the University of New Mexico Women's Resource Center in 1999. We used the activity in support groups for women students, focusing on body image, identity, and gender roles. I've recently been giving a lot of thought to group activities for mixed heritage kids, and crafted this adaptation of the exercise for use with this population.

Recommended readings:

Benedetto, A. E., & Olisky, T. (2001). Biracial youth: The role of the school counselor in racial identity development. *Professional School Counseling, 5*, 66-69.
Harris, H. L. (2002). School counselors' perceptions of biracial children: A pilot study. *Professional School Counseling, 6*, 120-129.
Herring, R. D. (1992). Biracial children: An increasing concern for elementary and middle school counselors. *Elementary School Guidance and Counseling, 27*, 123-130.
Nishimura, N. J. (1995). Addressing the needs of biracial children: An issue for counselors in a multicultural school environment. *The School Counselor, 43*, 52-57.
Root, M. P. P. (Ed.). (1996). *The multiracial experience.* Thousand Oaks, CA: Sage.
Wehrly, B., Kenny, K., & Kenney, M. (1999). *Counseling multiracial families.* Thousand Oaks, CA: Sage.

About the Group Worker:
Carmen F. Salazar, Ph.D., NCC, is an Associate Professor in the Department of Counseling at Texas A&M University-Commerce, Texas.

Rainbow Pride: Valuing Who I Am

Submitted by Anneliese A. Singh and Jolie Ziomek-Daigle

Goals:
- ✓ Provide a safe and supportive space for LGBT youth to talk about their identity
- ✓ Gain information about famous LGBT people from diverse backgrounds as positive models for LGBT youth

Target Population: Ages 14-18; LGBT adolescents from diverse backgrounds in school and community settings.

Potential Stage/Session(s): Orientation stage

Estimated Time Length: 50 minutes (or a class period)

Materials: No materials needed

Activity:
This activity includes four steps: (a) introducing LGBT youth to one another, (b) sharing what members appreciate or like about their LGBT identity, (c) identifying what they have in common with a famous LGBT person in history, and (d) sharing how they may use this commonality to deal with discrimination (e.g., bullying, violence).

Specific Directions for Activity:

✓ *Introducing LGBT youth to one another.*
This is the first and introductory step of the group. The facilitator welcomes the group members and affirms their participation and LGBT identity (e.g., "Appreciate that you have taken time to be here, as I value your LGBT identity and we will be creating a safe place to share with one another today"). Group members are invited to share their name, what they would like to get out of the group, and an extracurricular activity they enjoy. The facilitator introduces her/himself first in order to model the type and depth of sharing for group members.

✓ *Sharing what members appreciate or like about their LGBT identity.*
In the second step of the group, the leader facilitates a discussion about positive aspects of a LGBT identity. The facilitator asks members to list affirmative information they have heard, read, or think about having an LGBT identity. The facilitator keeps a list of these affirmative qualities, and then reads them aloud after everyone has finished sharing. Members are then asked to comment on which qualities they see in themselves.

✓ *Identifying what they have in common with a famous LGBT person in history.*
In the third step, the facilitator passes out large index cards with photos of famous LGBT people on one side of the card. On the back of the card, there are one to two sentences of brief information about the person's importance as an LGBT leader.

Suggestions for famous LGBT people to use are:

- ✓ Bayard Rustin (advisor to Dr. Martin Luther King, Jr.)
- ✓ Ellen Degeneres (talk show host)
- ✓ Christine Jorgensen (transgender woman)
- ✓ Ralph Waldo Emerson (writer)
- ✓ Barney Frank (U.S. Representative)
- ✓ Michael Stipe (singer)
- ✓ George Takei (actor on *Star Trek*)
- ✓ Joan Baez (singer)
- ✓ The Indigo Girls (band)

Guidelines for choosing these "models" should include the positive contributions they have made to LGBT people and society in general (*see web resource list below*). Members read off the information on the card and show the other members the photo. They discuss what they have in common with this person and/or what they can learn from this person's story to support developing a positive LGBT identity.

- ✓ *Sharing how they may use this commonality to deal with discrimination (e.g., bullying, violence).*

This final step is a closing activity. Group members are asked what they have learned about themselves and others in terms of feeling good about their LGBT identity. This step may be used to further discussion in the middle of the group, or it may be used as a check-out activity.

Processing Questions/Conclusion:
During the four steps of this group, facilitators may decide to follow up and ask members to expand strengths or barriers they experience in developing a positive LGBT identity. Also, facilitators may ask other members to comment as relevant to brainstorm how to respond to challenges of developing a positive LGBT identity (e.g., bullying).

The following process questions may be used throughout the four steps of the group. Facilitators are encouraged to ask members what words they would like to use to describe their identity. "LGBT" is used in this group entry, but this term may not be relevant for youth. It is important for facilitators to use terms and language that are preferred by group members.

- ✓ What thoughts and feelings come up for you as you hear people share about feeling good about their LGBT identity?
- ✓ What thoughts and feeling about feeling challenged about their LGBT identity?
- ✓ What types of people and situations support you in feeling good about your LGBT identity?
- ✓ What types of people and situations do you wish you didn't have to deal with because they make you feel badly about yourself as a LGBT person?

Cautions:
Working with LGBT youth requires familiarity and competence with the following: developmental theories, LGBT identity theories, intersection of LGBT identity with other identity developmental models (e.g., race/ethnicity, disability). It is also important for group facilitators to be aware of the degree of support and encouragement they have or need from the leaders in their school or community setting in order to ensure the safety and success of this group. Finally, LGBT youth may not be "out" to their peers, so ongoing reminders about the importance and limits of group confidentiality are critical.

Additional Comments:
Facilitators may consider inviting youth who are LGBT-allies into this type of group if that would be appropriate to the setting and/or goals of the group.

About the Group Workers:
Dr. Singh is on the editorial board of the *Journal for Specialists in Group Work* and has published on feminist group work interventions with survivors of trauma.

Dr. Ziomek-Daigle , LPC, RPT-S, is a former School Counselor with New Orleans Public Schools and a current faculty member at The University of Georgia.

The Write Words
Submitted by Elisabeth Liles

Goals:
- ✓ Encourage self-exploration
- ✓ Promote creativity
- ✓ Improve communication skills

Target Population: Ages 11-18; Students who have trouble expressing themselves

Potential Stage/Session(s): Any stage or session

Estimated Time Length: 30 minutes for activity and process discussion

Materials: A large pile of miscellaneous single words cut out of magazines and other resources, construction paper, glue sticks or tape

Activity: Students combine words from magazines to create a story about their day, their week, or their lives (choose one before the activity). The words are glued onto a large piece of construction paper. Students are then invited to share their stories with the group.

Specific Directions for Activity:
School counselor may begin with "Sometimes it is difficult to answer when someone asks you to tell about your day or about yourself. Either you do not know where to start, or you may not know what details to include. Having a prompt can help you get started. The purpose of this activity is to help students find a way to share something about themselves using someone else's words. In the process, students will explore their own sense of finding "the right words" to describe who they are."

Provide students with time to create their stories, and then allow them to share their stories with the group.
- ✓ Place the pile of words in the center of the group and provide each student with a piece of construction paper and a glue stick or tape
- ✓ Invite students to use the words to create a story about either their day, their week, or their lives
- ✓ Encourage students to choose as many words as they need to create their story, and that they can change or add words as they wish
- ✓ Students then glue their words onto the construction paper to be shared with the group

Processing Questions/Conclusion:
- ✓ How did you decide what words to use in creating your story?
- ✓ How was it different to use words that already existed than coming up with your own words?
- ✓ What did you do if you could not find a word you were looking for?
- ✓ How did you decide how to organize the words in your story?
- ✓ What emotion words did you choose to include in your story? If you do not have any emotion words, where could you include one?

Cautions:
Take care to select appropriate words based on age level, student characteristics, and school/community norms.

Additional Comments:
Variations on this activity include the following:
- ✓ Students can work together to create one story about the group members
- ✓ Use pictures instead of words
- ✓ Allow students to cut the words out of magazines

About the Group Worker:
Elisabeth Liles is a high School Counselor and a doctoral student in the Counselor Education and Supervision program at the University of Nevada, Reno.

Up, Up, and Away!

Submitted by Emily Karcher

Goals:
- ✓ To express thoughts and feelings toward a loved one who has died
- ✓ To understand that we all have unfinished business when we lose someone we love
- ✓ To participate in an activity with others who are experiencing grief and share in this common exercise

Target population: 10 years and up

Potential Stage/Session: Termination

Estimated Time: 45 minutes

Materials:
- ✓ One helium filled balloon for each group member
- ✓ Non-acetate markers

Activity: Give each member a helium filled balloon and allow each to choose markers to write on the balloon any thoughts or feelings that they would like to express to their deceased loved one. For example, members could write a happy memory, a current accomplishment, recent news, or any emotion they would like to express. Typically, members write "I love you," "I miss you," "You are my hero," "I passed my algebra final!," etc. After everyone is finished, the group goes outside and releases the balloons, shouting anything they wish as the balloons are lifted on high.

Processing Questions/Conclusion:

- ✓ How did it feel to write your feelings on your balloon?
- ✓ How did it feel to watch your balloon sail off into the sky?
- ✓ What feelings toward your loved one did you experience?
- ✓ Was this a joyful experience? Sad?
- ✓ Why is it a good idea to express unfinished business with our loved ones who have died?

About the Group Worker:
Emily Karcher, M.A., is a licensed School Counselor in Lakewood, Ohio.

Faces of a Stranger
Submitted by Tina R. Paone

Goals:
- ✓ Understand why people sometimes hide behind facades
- ✓ Assist students in understanding what facades are and why people use them
- ✓ How facades can affect students' lives.

Target population: Ages 11-18

Potential Stage/Session(s): Transition stage

Estimated Time Length: 30-40 minutes

Materials: Plastic/Paper masks (either cut outs or purchased), glue, paint (be sure to include multicultural color paints), various arts and crafts materials (e.g., feathers, beads, glitter, pom poms), and copy of the lyrics to "The Stranger."

Activity: This activity uses music and a mixed media craft to explore the use of interpersonal facades, or masks. Students are given an opportunity to explore the impact of failing to be true to their own values and sense of self.

Specific Directions for Activity:

The group facilitator will begin the group by presenting the following story. "One day you decide to wear red to school. You wear red because you like the color red and it is your school color. You go about your daily business and all of a sudden a group of people jump you and start beating you up. They think that you are in an opposing gang. During the scuffle, it is made apparent that you are not a member of an opposing gang, so the gang members stop beating you up and walk away. You decide that you will no longer wear red to school, even though it is your favorite color and it makes you happy." Students are left to ponder this story while the facilitator introduces the activity.

Students then listen to the Billy Joel song lyrics "The Stranger." Students are asked to think about the actions of the student as well as what happened to him/her in the story while listening to the song.

After they listen to the lyrics, students are asked to think about times when they did not represent themselves for who they are, but presented a "mask" to others. Students are supplied with a copy of the lyrics to this song.

After silent review of the lyrics, shift the group's attention back to the original story with the following questions.
- ✓ What would you do?
- ✓ Why would you make that decision?
- ✓ How does it affect you if you do tell someone?
- ✓ How does it affect those who beat you up?
- ✓ How does it affect if you if don't tell?

- ✓ How does it affect those who beat you up if you don't tell?
- ✓ How does your decision affect other students in the school?
- ✓ What in your life can you relate closely to this situation?
- ✓ What other events or situations are similar to this situation?
- ✓ Can you think of some examples that would cause you to think differently from what you would do in this specific example?
- ✓ What is the most important thing you consider when making decisions like this?
- ✓ Whose feelings do you consider when making tough decisions?

Students are instructed to create a mask for themselves using the plastic/paper mask and various supplies. No other specific direction is given. If students question, the counselor will respond "you get to decide" allowing total freedom of expression to the students.

Processing Questions/Conclusion:

Processing follows the creation of the mask. The following prompts may be used to stimulate discussion:
- ✓ Why does your mask look the way that it does?
- ✓ How does your mask represent who you are?
- ✓ How does your mask make you act differently?
- ✓ How does acting differently affect you?
- ✓ How does it affect those around you? Does your mask provide protection? From what or whom?
- ✓ Can you think of a time in your life where you have felt like you were wearing a mask? Talk about that time.

Homework:

Students are asked to take home their masks and share them with their friends and family. By sharing their mask, the introduction to a discussion dealing with facades can begin. It is important to remember the intensity of a discussion will depend on the student and relationship with whom he/she chooses to share the mask.

Cautions:
This activity can bring up very sensitive issues for students. It is important to remember to follow through with each topic that is brought to light. It is also important to remember that the processing questions presented here are only a guideline. All groups are different therefore, it is important to be flexible during processing allowing students to touch upon issues which they feel are important.

About the Group Worker:
Tina R. Paone, Ph.D., NCC, NCSC, RPT, is an Assistant Professor and Clinical Practicum/Internship Coordinator for the Educational Counseling Program at Monmouth University.

A Stone's Life

Submitted by Christine Lamke and Paula McWhirter

Goals:
- ✓ Express feelings related to changing family systems
- ✓ Identify how roles have changed as one's family has changed
- ✓ Increase cooperative behavior within the group

Target population: Ages 12-18

Potential Stage/Session(s): Working stage

Estimated Time Length: 30 - 45 minutes

Materials:
- ✓ One small, smooth stone for each group member. They can be easily purchased at craft stores or acquired from appropriate places in nature.
- ✓ Charles Simic's poem, *Stone,* one copy for each group member

Activity:
In this activity, a poem describing the life of a stone is used to help group members express feelings and gain insight about changes in the family. The stone metaphor helps students to understand thoughts and feelings about new family roles.

Introduction to Activity:
Tell students that in order to think about their changing family roles they are going to read a poem. Explain the concept of metaphor. Introduce this poem by explaining that the author is musing on life using the metaphor of stone. Explain that the speaker is thinking about what life would seem like if he were to be a stone and aware of life.

Invite students to choose a stone to hold and read the poem silently. Read the poem aloud and discuss how it may have sounded differently than when they first read it. You may take this opportunity to talk about the differences between rhyming poems and this particular style of poetry.

Students next respond in writing to the processing questions below. Conduct verbal group processing for each question. Depending on the group make-up and literacy level, it may be more useful to process after each question, rather than complete all written questions and then verbally process. Allow students to take their stones as a reminder of the information they have gained and their ability to be aware of the changes they are experiencing.

Processing Questions/Conclusion:

✓ Why would it be good to be a stone, rather than a dove or an animal brave enough to fight a tiger?

✓ A stone can handle all the pressure of a heavy animal stepping on it full force. What pressures have you silently bared as your family has changed?

✓ Children throw stones carelessly. When have you felt cast aside?

✓ The stone finds solace in the river bottom. Where do you find peace now that things have changed within your family?

✓ The fish listens to the stone. Who listens to you when you need to talk about important feelings/thoughts?

✓ There is light inside a stone, even though some people don't see through the rough exterior. Who sees your inner light?

✓ Who do you wish saw your inner light, but doesn't yet?

✓ What important hopes and secrets are written on your inner wall?

Cautions:

School counseling groups do not take the place of therapeutic treatment for trauma., loss, or Post Traumatic Stress Disorder. This group should be used to serve as an augment to such treatment as a way to aid students with their abilities to handle their responsibilities as students and as members of their social communities.

Credit/References:

Simic, C. (1999). Stone. In Charles Simic: *Selected Early Poems* (p. 39). New York: George Braziller Publishers.

About the Group Workers:

Christine Lamke is a graduate student at the University of Oklahoma and recently acquired her Master's in Education with a specialization in School Counseling.

Paula T. McWhirter, Ph.D., is an Assistant Professor of Counseling Psychology at the University of Oklahoma.

The Mock Career Fair
Submitted by Kelly Duncan, Seth Olson, and Christopher Roseman

Goals:
- ✓ Investigate and gather information on the career field of interest to the student
- ✓ Share and present information to other students who are beginning to explore careers
- ✓ Increase general career awareness and confidence in one's ability to manage career-related information

Target population: Ages 14-18; Individuals attending the culminating Mock Career Fair could be Middle School age.

Potential Stage/Session(s): Any stage or session

Estimated Time Length: One-Two Hours (depending on number of individuals attending)

Materials: Computer access, Power Point or other presentation software, poster boards

Activity: Prior to the day of the Career Fair group members need to research and investigate a career of their choosing and prepare a presentation on that career area to be shared at the Career Fair. Information could be formatted to be shared either as a Power Point presentation or as a Poster Presentation.

Hosting the Career Fair
Individuals can either set up their presentations around a large area or use a more formalized setting. They will present their power points/poster boards to their audience and then allow for questions.

Specific Directions for Activity:
1. Insure group members have completed an investigation in a career and prepared a presentation on their chosen career topic.
2. Allow students to share presentations briefly with a partner.
3. Set up for Career Fair.
4. Following Career Fair have group members journal their reflections on the day or do so as a group at the next group meeting.

Processing Questions/Conclusion:
(As a follow up to the activity individuals could either respond in the next group session or through a journaling activity to the following questions.)

1. As you reflect upon this activity, what surprised you most about the career that you chose to investigate?
2. With the information you have gained, what are your thoughts about pursuing a career in the area studied?
3. After completing this activity, what have you learned about your abilities related to gathering information and presenting it to others?
4. What do you see as your next steps in your career journey?

Cautions:
This group experience assumes that individuals participating have completed some career exploration prior to beginning the activity. If not, a prior career exploration activity may be necessary. The activity may need to be altered if computer access is not available or the ability to create Power Point presentations not possible.

About the Group Workers:
Dr. Kelly Duncan is a former School Counselor and is currently an Assistant Professor in the Department of Counseling at the University of South Dakota, Vermillion, where she serves as the School Counseling Program Coordinator.

Dr. Seth Olson is an Assistant Professor in the Department of Counseling at the University of South Dakota, Vermillion.

Dr. Christopher P. Roseman, LPC, NCC, is an Assistant Professor in the Counseling Program at the University of South Dakota where he serves as the Clinical Director for the campus Counseling and Family Therapy Center.

Career Information Power Point Outline

Based on the information that you gathered while researching your career, you will prepare a Power Point or poster presentation. The outline below shows the areas that need to be covered.

Job Title

Brief Job Description

Employment Facts about Career
      Approximate number of jobs in nation
      Settings
      Range of salary
      Full or part time

Educational requirements for career
      High school courses needed for solid preparation
      Post secondary training requirements
      Post secondary institutions offering training

Other pertinent requirements for career (experience, certifications)

Advancement opportunities in career field

Job outlook for career

Briefly describe a day in the life of the chosen career

Related careers and/or resources re: career field

Surprising facts/information about this career

Tips for Creating a Power Point Presentation
- Use a standard font—fancy fonts can be hard to read
- Use only 6 words per line/6 lines per slide
- Font size should range from 20 to 48 point
- Know your audience and use appropriate language

Website Resources for Facilitator

Career Assessments for Fee

Self-Directed Search (Interest Inventory):
www.self-directed-search.com

Choices (Interest Inventory):
www.bridges.com

Kuder Occupational Interest Survey:
www.kuder.com

Strong-Campbell Interest Inventory:
www.pearsonassessments.com/tests/ciss

Free Career Assessments

Free Career Test   www.questcareer.com

Free Career Assessment   www.livecareer.com

The Career Key   www.careerkey.org

Additional Resources and Websites for Career Development

Kapes, J.T., & Whitfield, E.A. (2001). *A Counselor's guide to career assessment instruments*. Alexandria, VA: ACA

Career Assessment Tools and Tests   www.quintcareers.com/career_assessment

Dictionary of Occupational Titles   www.occupationalinfo.org

Bureau of Labor Statistics   http://www.bls.gov/k12/

Department of Labor   http://www.dol.gov/

Career Tests and Job Planning   www.careerpath.com

Managing School Transitions

Submitted by Debbie Vernon

Goals:
- ✓ Identify the impact of transitions in four areas: (a) roles; (b) relationships with others; (c) routines; and (d) assumptions/expectations.
- ✓ Identify individual reactions to the transition and assess available coping resources that may be useful during the transition process
- ✓ Learn to take charge of the transition by strengthening coping resources and putting new strategies to use

Target Populations: Ages 10-18
Specific Transitions:
- ✓ Students transitioning into middle school
- ✓ Students transitioning into high school
- ✓ Students transitioning into college
- ✓ Parent Group for any of the above student categories

Potential Stage/Session(s): Orientation or transition stage

Estimated Time Length: 1 class period (55 - 90 minutes)

Materials:
- ✓ Writing utensils, paper, markers, and crayons to assist with drawing pictures of the transition, its impact, my coping responses, and new strategies.
- ✓ See processing questions for activities that can be made into handouts for any age group or for parent group.
- ✓ A dry erase board or flip chart is helpful for summarizing group responses to processing activities.

Activity:
This is a strength-based group that helps students and/or parents focus on what is working, what is not working, and what they want to be able to do differently to help them navigate transition successfully. It is important to normalize transitions and change as a part of life. The leader provides examples of possible impacts of change and ideas about resources. Group members are reminded that the coping skills they have used in navigating past life transitions can help them with the present situation. This group is particularly useful at the beginning of a transition, such as the beginning semester of a school year or the end of a school year.

Specific Directions for Activity:
Identify the specific transition that the group is commonly facing and normalize how all people react to transition in some way. Introduce concepts and provide examples. Explain that coping well with transition requires a personal assessment of the following:

a) What is the situation and-or transition and its characteristics
b) What characteristics do I have that can be helpful during a time of transition
c) What supportive relationships or connections do I have available to me in a time of need
d) What strategies and-or responses do I have access to that may be useful during stressful situations.

Break the large group into smaller groups to build cohesion to discuss processing questions.

Processing Questions/Conclusion:
- ✓ Assess the impact of change. Where are the greatest changes? Which areas are hardest for me right now?
    - o New roles
    - o New routines
    - o New relationships
    - o New expectations/assumptions
- ✓ Assess strengths and resources available to me. What (if any) area(s) do I need the most help with right now? (4-S's)
    - o My situation
    - o My supports
    - o My self
    - o My strategies or tools
- ✓ What are my options? What decisions are available to me? Which of the 4-S's do I want to address right now to help me manage this transition?
    - o Do I want to change my "S"? (taking action)
    - o Do I want to change the way I view my "S"? (using my knowledge and skills)
    - o Do I want to change the way I manage my "S" even if I can't change it or change the way I see it? (reaction management)
    - o Do I want to do nothing and just keep the "status quo"?
- ✓ What do I want to do? Explain why.
- ✓ What plan of action can you make right now?

Reconvene to larger group for sharing of learning about self and others from processing activities (a) and (b). Foster connections by linking group members to each other through similarities in responses. For final activity (c), individuals work alone to respond to the processing questions and development of action plan. Offer opportunities to share individual plans with the large group.

The school counselor can provide support and encouragement to individual members as they make plans for the present and future. Remind members of the role of school counselor as an additional support to individual members during their school experience.

Credit/References:
Chickering, A. W., & Schlossberg, N.K. (1995). *Getting the most out of college.* Boston: Allyn & Bacon.

Schlossberg, N. K., Waters, E. B., & Goodman, J. (1995). *Counseling adults in transition* (2nd ed.). New York: Springer.

I first learned about Transition Theory while working on my dissertation. This activity was based on a single-session group program I developed which focused on helping first year college students manage the transition to college. Since then, I have used this approach with my middle school groups I conduct, modifying the developmental level as needed.

Cautions:
For younger age groups or students identified as having specific learning disabilities, modifications may need to be made in the terminology used. For example, the notion of "transition" can be modified to "changes," and the term "resources" can be modified to "tools."

About the Group Worker:
Dr. Debbie Vernon is a Professional School Counselor and Internship Supervisor at Hudson Middle School in Hudson, Ohio and part-time instructor in the Department of Educational Foundations and Special Services at Kent State University.

Identifying Your Family Role
Submitted by Jillian Abram

Goals:
- ✓ Identify one's possible family role
- ✓ Identify and express feelings about family roles
- ✓ Consider how one's family role may change in the future

Target population: Ages 14-18; Students who may be coping with family issues (i.e., children of divorce, children of substance abusers).

Potential Stage/Session(s): Working stage

Estimated Time Length: 30-45 minutes

Materials: Family Roles handout, Family Roles worksheet, pen or pencil

Activity:
Ask students what comes to their minds when you mention the word "family." For many, it will be people, such as parents or siblings. But for some, the word family may cause them to think of feelings, such as anger or joy, or situations, such as a current conflict, a busy schedule, or a vacation. Communicate to the group that each student's thoughts about family are going to be unique and somewhat different from everyone else's in the group. How and where students see themselves fitting into their family will vary as well. Give students an opportunity to share what they thought of when the word "family" was spoken.

Specific Directions for Activity:
- ✓ Introduce the activity (The handout and worksheet provided are intended to spark discussion about the group members' families and family roles. Specific directions are flexible and should be adjusted as needed.)
- ✓ Hand out the description of Family Roles. Have the group members read through the descriptions, either silently or aloud. Facilitate a discussion about the roles and which roles the group members identify with.
- ✓ Pass out the Family Roles worksheet. Have the group members answer the questions on the worksheet. Use the questions and students' answers as a springboard for more discussion about family roles.
- ✓ Conclude by encouraging students to discuss their recorded thoughts with at least one person in their family.

Processing Questions/Conclusion:
- ✓ See Family Roles worksheet for processing questions.
- ✓ In a future session, discuss healthy ways to handle family changes and have students make a plan of how they want to deal with a known upcoming change

Cautions:
This activity could cause students to become defensive and/or unwilling to "label" themselves. It is important to emphasize that the role descriptions are generalizations; even if a student identifies with a certain family role, it does not necessarily mean that every quality applies to that student.

Credit/References:
The Family Roles handout was adapted from the book *Another Chance: Hope and Health for the Alcoholic Family* by Sharon Wegscheider-Cruse. Although the family roles in the book were written about a chemically dependent family, the descriptions apply to any family with dysfunctional patterns.

Wegscheider-Cruse, S. (1981). *Another chance: Hope and health for the alcoholic family.* Palo Alto, CA: Science and Behavior Books.

About the Group Worker:
Jillian Abram recently earned her Master of Arts in Counselor Education from the University of Central Florida.

FAMILY ROLES

FAMILY HERO: Sensitive and caring. Feeling responsible for the pain of the family, the Hero tries to improve the situation. The Hero strives for success, but because the family does not change, he or she ultimately feels like a failure.

SCAPEGOAT: Opposite of the Hero. The Scapegoat tries to gain recognition by pulling away in a destructive manner, bringing negative attention to self by getting in trouble, getting hurt, or just withdrawing. (Note: Any attention is better than being ignored.)

LOST CHILD: Offers relief to the family by taking care of his or her own problems and needs. Isolates and avoids trouble. The family ignores the child. This inattention results in loneliness and depression.

SICK CHILD: Finds acceptance in being ill, the only path that feels available for attention and compassion.

MASCOT: Provides relief and humor for the family by being charming and funny during stressful times. This humor does not help the Mascot deal with personal pain and loneliness.

Source: Sharon Wegscheider-Cruse (1981)

Questions about *Your* Family Role

What is one role you play in your family?

What do you like about your current family role?

What do you *not* like about your current family role?

How does your current role make you feel?

What role would you like to have in your family?

How do you think your role may change over the next year?

How do you think this new or different role would make you feel?

You've Got Mail!

Submitted by Amy Brown, Amber Lange and Marie Horton

Goals:
- ✓ Increase knowledge about communication in peer relationships
- ✓ Learn positive methods of dealing with opposite sex relationships

Target population: Ages 12-14; Most effective with girls

Potential Stage/Session(s): Working stage

Estimated Time Length: 40-50 minutes, 1-2 Sessions

Materials: A large index card or notebook paper; a plastic mail box or a covered box with a slit cut out of the lid (similar to a mail box); examples of "Dear Abby" type letters

Activity: At the end of a session prior to implementing the You've Got Mail activity, ask the students to write an anonymous letter requesting advice about a peer or dating relationship problem. As part of this discussion, give a small background about anonymous advice column letters that are often seen in the newspaper. Use an example of this type of letter in order to help the students understand how they may want to write their own letters. Explain to the students that each letter will be seen by their peers in the group, but the authors of the letters will remain anonymous. Once they have finished writing a letter, have them place the letter in the mail box. These letters will be saved in the school counselor's office until the next group session. Plan to allot 5-10 minutes to complete this part of the activity.

Prior to the next session, preview the letters for appropriateness, etc. If you find an inappropriate letter, you will have to replace the inappropriate letter with another one. At the next session, explain to the students that they are going to have a chance at being an advice columnist. Pass out a letter to each girl in the group. Ask them to take a few minutes to read the letter and to try to think about some possible solutions to the issue. Then have each student write a letter of advice back to the person who wrote the original letter. Allow 10-15 minutes for this portion of the activity.

After everyone has finished writing the new advice letter, have the students begin presenting the advice to the group. One at a time, have the student read the letter asking for advice to the group, then have the student read the response. After each letter is read, process the advice letter with the discussion questions below.

Processing Questions/Conclusion:
- ✓ What do you feel about the advice?
- ✓ How could these ideas be implemented at home? School?
- ✓ Would anyone do anything different in this situation? If so, explain.
- ✓ Was the advice you gave based on personal experience? If not, how did you come to your conclusion about what advice to give? If so, how did the advice work in your situation?
- ✓ In what ways might you try this advice before the next session?

Cautions:

The counselor must screen the letters for age appropriate content, for issues that may not be appropriate for group work, and for content that does not apply to dating or relationship issues. By asking the participants to write the questions before the processing session, the counselor has more time to preview the questions.

This activity will be most useful for students who were carefully selected to fit into a peer/dating relationship group. It is important for the school counselor to consider the students' developmental age and degree of similar experiences as students of middle school age range likely will have varied experiences with the opposite sex. Thus, to have a sexually experienced student give dating advice to a sexually inexperienced student may be damaging to the participants and damaging to the group in general.

Additional Comments:

It is important that the counselor previewing the questions be able to tell which questions belong to each participant if issues arise that may be inappropriate for group and may need to be handled in individual counseling. Examples include questions about personal dating violence, suicidal thoughts, or disclosure of current sexual activity.

Credit/References:

Myers, S.E., Syers, H.A., Voyer, S.D., Thurlow, J.L., Cohen, J.N., & Weaver, A.D. (2003). An adolescent perspective on sexual health education at school and at home: II. Middle school students. *The Canadian Journal of Human Sexuality, 12*(1), 19-33.

McKay, A., & Holowaty, P. (1997). Sexual health education: A study of adolescents' opinions, self-perceived needs, and current and preferred sources of information. *Canadian Journal of Human Sexuality, 6*, 29-38.

About the Group Workers:

Amy Brown, M.A., FS, is a high school teacher and current student in the Community Counseling program at Spring Arbor University in Michigan.

Amber Lange, LPC, is a licensed counselor in Michigan and doctoral candidate in the Counselor Education program at the University of Toledo in Ohio.

Marie Horton, M.A., is a special education teacher in Toledo, Ohio and is currently completing an additional master's degree in Counseling at Spring Arbor University, Spring Arbor, MI.

Red Flag

Submitted by Barbara C. Trolley and Andrew Mattle

Goals:
- ✓ Identify risky situations (e.g., alcohol, drugs, sexual victimization, health issues-STD's)
- ✓ Explore one's own perceptions of risk and values related to risky situations
- ✓ Develop strategies to avoid risky situations
- ✓ Receive peer support for coping with risky situations

Target Population: Ages 13-18; Break into two developmental age groups whenever possible

Potential Stage/Session(s): Transition or working stage

Estimated Time Length: 30 minutes, depending on group size

Materials:
- ✓ Pens, pencils, markers
- ✓ Red construction paper

Activity:
This activity uses the creation of a "red flag" to illustrate the danger students may experience in situations that put them at risk for physical or emotional harm or legal problems. Through processing the creation of a red flag, each group member may identify risky situations they have or might encounter and begin to develop strategies for maintaining personal safety and integrity.

Specific Directions for Activity:
The group leader provides a context for the creation of a red flag. The following is an example of an introductory statement:

"The purpose of this activity is to assist each group member to identify specific situations they encounter which put them at physical, emotional or legal risk. It is an activity in which all members will have an opportunity to share their ideas, develop strategies to decrease risk potential for themselves, and learn from each other."

"Everyone will take one piece of red construction paper and draw a flag. Each flag must include a number of 'stripes'. On these stripe lines, list situations you have encountered or could encounter that would put you at risk physically, emotionally or legally. Please be as specific as possible. For example, instead of saying 'underage drinking' a member may state that drinking X number of drinks at a party of boys and girls present, few of them who are friends, most are acquaintances, in a deserted park area."

"As you make the list, think of not only physical surroundings, but your own mood, (are you more likely to take a risk if you are angry), and thought patterns (i.e., if you are really down on yourself)."

Allow group members time to silently reflect and create their list. Then ask the group to silently consider what has prevented them from avoiding that risk in the future. Are they ready to consider ways to decrease the risks they take?

Processing Questions/Conclusion:
The following are examples of processing questions that might be used to explore the topic:
- ✓ What situations put you at the highest/least risk and why?
- ✓ What are the specific risks that might be encountered in any one situation?
- ✓ What triggers, (i.e., moods, thoughts, circumstances, friends) are apt to influence you to be in these risky situations?
- ✓ What is the impact of some of these risky situations to you?
- ✓ How can you decrease risk to yourself?
- ✓ What is in your control and what isn't to change?

Cautions:
Be careful to keep the focus on avoiding, rather than sharing ideas about, risky situations. Make sure that coping strategies to eliminate risk are addressed, not just the identification of situations.

Additional Comments:
This group activity was originally developed this for teen survivors of sexual abuse (incest and extra familial abuse). This activity can be used as an intervention with teens experiencing other types of trauma., with additional cautions specific to the presenting concern. The activity can also be used as a preventative tool for all teens.

About the Group Workers:
Barbara C. Trolley, Ph.D., CRC, is an Associate Professor in Counselor Education at St. Bonaventure University.

Andrew Mattle, MSED, LMHC, is Director of Mental Health Services AIDS Community Services of WNY Inc.

Family Feud
Submitted by Jake J. Protivnak

Goals:
- ✓ Practice and reinforce knowledge learned during earlier group sessions
- ✓ Develop teamwork among members
- ✓ Practice following directions in a group setting
- ✓ Demonstrate appropriate impulse control

Target Population: Ages 11-14

Potential Stage/Session(s): Working or termination stage

Estimated Time Length: 30 minutes (can be extended)

Materials:
Flip chart on an easel, adhesive tape, large index cards, three index cards with a red X drawn on each, two bells (or other signaling devices), questions and answers to material covered in the group, and three tables

Activity:
The group leader leads an activity based upon the popular television game show "Family Feud." This will include developing questions and multiple answers based upon the information shared by the group leader and the knowledge group members learned during the previous group sessions.

This activity can be used to reinforce the knowledge learned with a variety of different group topics (academic, career, and personal/social skill topics). Students who are talkative, energetic, and committed to learning the group material may particularly enjoy this activity.

Specific Directions for Activity:
Similar to the television show "Family Feud," the leader will identify several questions regarding material covered during the group and multiple answers for each questions.

Pregroup Preparation
The leader writes the first question on the top of the flip chart and the multiple answers underneath the question. Additional questions and matching answers can be written on subsequent pages on the flip chart. The leader will cover each answer on each page of the paper flip chart with a separate large index card taped over the answer. The leader will have an answer sheet with a list of the questions and all of the answers.

The leader arranges the room to have two tables set up across from each other and one table at the head of the room. The leader will set up the bells on opposite ends of the table at the front of the room. The flip chart with questions and answers will be set on the easel at the front of the room.

Activity Instructions

Group members are divided into two separate teams. The group members in each team select a team name, write the name on a piece of paper and tape it to the front of their table. The group members organize themselves into who will go first, second, third, and so forth. On their turn, each group member comes forward to the head table, stands in front of the bell (or signaling device), and listens to the question read.

The leader explains the activity to the group members. The group leader instructs each team to have one group member come forward. The group members come to the front of the room and each stand at opposite ends of the table in front of the bell (or signaling device).

The leader reads the question at the top of the flip chart. The first student who rings the bell (or signaling devise) will have the opportunity to provide an answer to the question. If the student answers the question correctly, then the leader goes to the team members and allows the team members to provide additional answers to the question until the three wrong answers are given. If three wrong answers are given and a correct answer is still on the board, then the leader goes to the other team. The other team will discuss and together, present an answer to match the covered answer on the flip chart.

Each time a team member gives a correct answer, that team receives a point. If a group member provides an answer not listed on the poster board or is unable to provide an answer, the group receives a strike. After receiving three strikes, the other team has an opportunity to provide an answer to the question. The team with the most points at the end of the game wins the activity.

Processing Questions/Conclusion:
This activity includes specific questions based upon the material already presented in the group. For example, a question for a career-focused group might be, "What are the most common ways to find information about specific jobs?"

Process questions at the end of the activity can include the following:
   ✓ How well did your group work together as a team?
   ✓ How did you handle the frustration of not answering the question correctly or not winning the activity?
   ✓ Based on your performance in this activity, how well do you know the material that we have discussed in this group?
   ✓ Share an instance during the activity when you could have behaved inappropriately, but instead controlled your impulse. How did you do that?

Cautions:
Select questions that are neither too hard nor too difficult, but based upon the material covered in the group. This activity requires preparation by the group leader prior to the activity to write the questions and answers on the flip chart, gather materials, and set up the group room.

Additional Comments:
This activity can be used to reinforce the knowledge learned with a variety of different group topics (Academic, Career, & Personal/Social Skill topics). Students who are talkative, energetic, and committed to learning the group material may particularly enjoy this activity.

Credit/References:
This group activity was successfully led with a group of students who were diagnosed with ADHD. The questions and answers used within the "Family Feud" activity focused on the academic and study skills of the students. The co-leader of the group was Dr. Laura Bruneau, who is currently an Assistant Professor in the Counseling program at Adams State College.

About the Group Worker:
Jake J. Protivnak, Ph.D., PCC-S, LSC, NCC, is currently an Assistant Professor in the Department of Counseling and Special Education at Youngstown State University with primary teaching responsibilities in School Counseling.

Generation Y and Technology: What's Going on?

Submitted by Holly Nikels and Kelly Duncan

Goals:
- ✓ Inform parents about on-line safety practices and the prevention of cyber-bullying
- ✓ Assist parents in understanding how they can better help their children cope with risks associated with new technology

Target population: Parents of middle and high school aged students

Potential Stage/Session(s): Any stage or session

Estimated Time Length: Two hours

Materials: LCD Projector for PowerPoint, handouts, computer(s), internet connection

Activity: The following topics are presented in a psychoeducational format:
- ✓ Who is Generation Y?
- ✓ Definition, Values and Influences
- ✓ What is Cyberbullying? (Bullying vs. Cyberbullying, Forms of Cyberbullying: Cell phones/ Text messages, Instant messages/E-mails)
- ✓ Social networking sites
  - o Interactive on-Line demonstrations
- ✓ Technology 101- definitions
- ✓ Facebook/ MySpace demonstration
  - o Handout: Cyberbullying – Warning Signs
- ✓ Tips for Parents
- ✓ Prevention/ Intervention strategies: Family computer safety plan
  - o Handout: Online Safety
- ✓ Resources
  - o Resource list

Specific Directions for Activity:
- a. Introduce the content on internet usage and potential dangers.
- b. Present demonstration of on-line social networking sites.
- c. Discuss handouts on online safety.
- d. Conclude with processing questions. This one should be d instead of two c's.

Processing Questions/Conclusion:
- ✓ Why is it important to understand internet usage and safety issues?
- ✓ How can technology be harmful/dangerous to your child?
- ✓ How can technology be helpful to your child?
- ✓ How will you use this information to develop safe internet rules or practices with your child?

Cautions:
When doing the on-line demonstrations, be cautious about using the name of the city you are presenting in, or using the name of a local student for a search. It is impossible to predict what might be shown on-line, so in order to avoid embarrassment to a parent in the group, it is better to search more generally. Prior to the group session be sure that the internet blocks are removed or you will be unable to access the social networking sites. Consult with the school's technology staff for assistance with this.

Credit/References:
Ehrecke, C., Jenkins, R., Lempke, K., Miller, S., Olsen S. & Sedlak, A.
        (2008) *Cyberbullying.what it is: How to keep it from
        happening: How to make it stop.* Unpublished manuscript.
Nikels, H.J. (2008). *Generation Y and technology: What is going on?* Unpublished
        manuscript.
Other citations noted on handouts

About the Group Workers:
Holly Nikels is a former School Counselor and an Associate Professor in the Department of Counselor Education at Western Illinois University.

Dr. Kelly Duncan is a former School Counselor and is currently an Assistant Professor in the Department of Counseling at the University of South Dakota in Vermillion, where she serves as the School Counseling Program Coordinator.

CYBERBULLYING: Warning Signs
By Sameer Hinduja, Ph.D. and Justin Patchin, Ph.D.

A child may be a victim of a cyberbully if he/she...	A child may be cyberbullying others if he/she...
• Unexpectedly stops using the computer	• Quickly switches screens or closes programs when you walk by
• Appears nervous or jumpy when an Instant Message or E-mail appears	• Uses the computer at all hours of the night
• Appears uneasy about going to school or outside in general	• Gets unusually upset if he or she cannot use the computer
• Appears to be angry, depressed or frustrated after using the computer	• Laughing excessively while using the computer
• Avoids discussions about what they are doing on the computer	• Avoids discussions about what they are doing on the computer
• Becomes abnormally withdrawn from usual friends and family members	• Is using multiple online accounts, or an account that is not their own

ON-LINE SAFETY:
PREVENTION AND INTERVENTION STRATEGIES FOR
PARENTS AND CAREGIVERS

- **Set up rules:**
  - Post clear, simple, easy to read rules on or near the monitor. Create your own computer rules or print out rules from on-line resources

- **Use filters:**
  - Consider using filtering or monitoring software for your computer. Look into safeguarding programs or options your on-line service provider might offer. Have your child use child friendly search engines when completing homework.

- **Check out privacy policies:**
  - Always read a website's privacy policy before you or your children provide any personal information. Also make sure the website offers a secure connection before giving credit-card information.

- **Talk about the dangers of e-mail and chat:**
  - If your children use chat or e-mail, talk to them about never meeting an on-line "friend" face to face. Talk to your child about not responding to offensive or dangerous e-mail, chat or other communication. Report such instances to local law enforcement.

- **Know what's going on:**
  - Keep the computer in the family room or another open area of your home. Let your child show you what they can do on-line, and visit their favorite sites or chat rooms with them.

- **Avoid over-reacting with harsh sanctions**
  - E.g., banning use of computer

On-Line Resources

Net Lingo:
> *This site contains thousands of definitions about computers, the Internet, and the online world of business, technology & communication.*
>> www.netlingo.com

Cyberbullying:
> *A central repository and information clearinghouse for the phenomenon of cyberbullying.*
>> www.cyberbullying.us

STOP Cyberbullying:
> *What cyberbullying is, how it works and how to understand and deal with cyberbullies.*
>> www.stopcyberbullying.org

NetSmartz:
> *Educational resource from the National Center for Missing & Exploited Children. Discusses various internet safety topics*
>> www.netsmartz.org

Net Family News:
> *A weekly electronic **news** service to inform and educate parents, families and caregivers of children who spend time online.*
>> www.netfamilynews.org

Safe Kids
> *Worldwide is a global network of organizations whose mission is to prevent accidental childhood injury, a leading killer of children 14 and under.*
>> www.safekids.org

McGruff the Crime Dog:
> *McGruff the Crime Dog and pal, Scruff, bring ideas about kids staying safe through safety puzzles, games, and coloring pages.*
>> www.mcgruff.org

National Crime Prevention Council:
>> www.ncpc.org

The Hot Seat
Submitted by Matthew Day

Goals:
- ✓ Build communication and conflict resolution skills by allowing adolescents to become more effective at giving and receiving corrective feedback
- ✓ Increase ability to address frustration with others prior to incidents of potential aggression
- ✓ Allow adolescents to become more aware of their own feelings about the actions of others and how to effectively communicate their feelings
- ✓ Help students differentiate between expressing themselves assertively and aggressively

Target population: Ages 12-18

Potential Stage/Session(s): Orientation or transition stage

Estimated Time Length: 30-45 minutes

Materials: No materials necessary, but it may be beneficial to have a squeezable ball or similar item which the person on the "hot seat" can hold while talking and then can toss to the person who decides to speak next

Activity: The group, including the leader, sits in a circle with a chair, the "hot seat," placed in the center. The leader can do a brief warm-up, introducing the activity as one that will help in giving and receiving feedback from each other.
Participants can be chosen to be in the "hot seat" in the following ways:
- ✓ Choose names from a hat (once a participant has been chosen, their name does not go back into the hat until all participants have been in the "hot seat" at least once;
- ✓ Take student volunteers (once again, all participants must have a turn before volunteering again); or
- ✓ Select students based upon a significant event, (i.e., a participant has been having some difficulties getting along with her/his peers)

Once a participant is in the "hot seat," the leader asks for members in the circle to express one way that this person has been helpful to them and one way that person has not been helpful to them over the last week. The leader can phrase questions in a variety of ways depending on what issues need to be worked on. The participant in the "hot seat" cannot respond to any of the feedback until all participants have spoken. Once all participants have spoken, the member in the "hot seat" rejoins the circle and processing questions begin.

Processing Questions/Conclusion: Questions will vary based upon the specifics of the population. The following questions may be beneficial:
To the participant in the "hot seat"
- ✓ How did it feel to hear some of the positive things about you being noticed and discussed?

150

✓ How did it feel to hear some of the corrective things about you being noticed and discussed?
✓ Discuss a time you wanted to respond to a specific statement and did not because of the boundaries of the group.

To the participants directing statements to the "hot seat"
✓ How did it feel being able to verbalize some feedback to the person in the "hot seat" knowing that he/she could not immediately respond to you?
✓ How did you feel as you listened to some of the others' statements of feedback that were given to the person in the "hot seat"?
✓ Was there a statement of feedback made that would have been difficult for you to hear had you been on the "hot seat" and for what reason?

Cautions:
Some comments may lead to frustration and anxiety. The member on the "hot seat" may feel attacked or anxious in regard to the feedback that has given, and may feel quite vulnerable. For these reasons, a check-in at the start of the group and check-out at the close of the group should occur to address these potential dynamics.

Additional Comments:
Each participant should be on the "hot seat"' on at least one occasion during the duration of this group process.

About the Group Worker:
Matthew S. Day, Ph.D. is an Assistant Professor in the Counselor Education Program, Educational and Community Programs at Queens College, CUNY, in Flushing, New York.

Cyberbullying Awareness

Submitted by Kelly Duncan and Holly Nikels

Goals:
- ✓ Inform participants about cyberbullying and appropriate/inappropriate online incidents
- ✓ Identify strategies for responding to cyberbullying

Target population: Ages 11-18

Potential Stage/Session(s): Any stage or session

Estimated Time Length: 45 minutes

Materials: *Case Scenarios* handout

Activity:

Introduce and explain cyberbullying. The following information would be presented as a starting point for further discussion by group members:

- ✓ What is cyberbullying?
- ✓ What should you do if you are a victim?
  - Talk to your parents or an adult
  - Save the evidence
  - Report incidents to your Internet service provider, e-mail provider, or Web site host. If the incidents begin occurring offline, report the encounters to the bully's parents or to school/law enforcement officials.

- ✓ Break into small groups to discuss the cyberbullying case scenarios for small group and larger group discussion (see handout)
- ✓ Conclude with processing questions as a large group.

Processing Questions/Conclusion:
- ✓ Why is it important to understand being safe while using the internet?
- ✓ What are some examples of cyberbullying and how can you avoid becoming a victim?
- ✓ What is your role in avoiding becoming a cyber bully?
- ✓ Share some of your group's discussion of the scenarios presented.

About the Group Workers:

Dr. Kelly Duncan is a former School Counselor and is currently an Assistant Professor in the Department of Counseling at the University of South Dakota in Vermillion, where she serves as the School Counseling Program coordinator.

Holly Nikels is a former School Counselor and is currently an Associate Professor in the Department of Counselor Education at Western Illinois University.

CYBERBULLYING
Case Scenarios

Directions: Read each of the following cases as a group. Then discuss how you would handle the situation if you were the person in the story.

Case 1
For over 2 weeks, Erica has found a daily message in her INBOX from someone with the name Not Telling You and the email address: nottellingyou@hotmail.com. The messages have been centered around telling her she is ugly, commenting about how horrible she looked in school today, or making a comment about something she has said in one of her classes. Erica has begun to dread turning on the computer and every day when she does she hopes that the emails will have stopped. She has tried responding to the sender asking what she has done to make them say such mean things to her and asking them to quit. The sender never responds to her emails, but instead just sends another one the next day with an even more hurtful message. Erica is afraid to tell her friends because she isn't sure if one of them might be sending the emails. She doesn't want to tell her parents because she is afraid they will make her stay off the computer. How do you think Erica should handle this situation?

Case 2
Mike recently put up a site on one of the social network sites that most of the kids in his school are using. He has added as many individuals to his friends list as would allow him to do so. Last week someone created a MIKE SMITH IS A LOSER group and invited most of the kids in his class to join. To his shock, many of his classmates have done so. What would you do if you were Mike?

Case 3
Kara has chosen to have an "honesty box" on her Facebook site. She is noticing that all of the anonymous postings to her honesty box are really negative. She doesn't feel good when she reads them and they are beginning to make her wonder which of her friends might be posting them. Kara finally confides in you as her best friend. What advice would you give Kara?

Friendship Gumbo Group

Submitted by Katrina Norris

Goals:
- ✓ Identify ideal characteristics of healthy friendships
- ✓ Describe elements that are important for building and maintaining a friendship
- ✓ Begin to apply material to one's own important relationships

Target Population: Ages 12-18

Potential Stage/Session(s): Any stage or session

Estimated Time Length: 30 minutes

Materials: Construction paper to create cut-out bowl, markers, tape, and relationship element list: Trust, loyalty, honesty, values, intelligence, compassion, money, and sense of style.

Activity: Friendship values and skills are emphasized in this activity. The metaphor of a recipe for a "perfect friendship gumbo" is used to identify important components of healthy peer relationships.

Specific Directions for Activity:
Prior to the activity, take time to process last week's activity. Take time to address any questions/thoughts group members may have. After discussing last week's activity, take time to ask student's if they have the perfect friendship. If a student feels they do, ask one student to talk about what in the friendship makes it perfect.

Once the student is done discussing their perfect friendship, ask each student to think about what elements make a perfect friendship. Group members should then write down his or her own recipe for the perfect friendship. Group members are encouraged to create a recipe using the relationship element list along with other important ingredients necessary for a perfect friendship.

An example of the recipe may be:
- ✓ One cup of trust
- ✓ One tablespoon of values
- ✓ A dash of intelligence.

Once each person has completed their own personal recipe, the entire group works together with the help of the group leader to create the "perfect friendship gumbo" with the help of the group leader. As the group is discussing the perfect recipe, the group leader writes the ingredients in the bowl to help create the "perfect friendship gumbo."

Processing Questions/Conclusion:
- ✓ How did you come up with the elements to include in their recipes?
- ✓ Looking at the final recipe, is there anything you would change about it?
- ✓ How different is the group recipe from your original recipe?

✓ Have you had any friendships comparable to that recipe? If yes, are there any flaws to that friendship? If not, do you think it is possible to have this perfect of a relationship?
✓ Do you think this recipe would change if you were talking about the perfect parent/perfect co-worker/perfect significant other? Why or why not?

In a closing round, invite group members to respond to the following question:
✓ What one thing did you learn from today's group that you plan to think about more in the coming week?

About the Group Worker:

Katrina Norris currently works in the mental health field with children and adolescents and is a recent graduate from the University at Buffalo, State University of New York with a Master's Degree in School Counseling.

The Torn Heart Treatment Team

Submitted by Adam P. Zagelbaum

Goals:
- ✓ Process experiences of sadness, pain, and anger
- ✓ Generate problem solving approaches to dealing with sadness, pain and anger
- ✓ Aid in building a feeling vocabulary
- ✓ Facilitate interpersonal communication regarding feelings and coping with difficult feelings

Target Population: Ages 11-18

Potential Stage/Session(s): Any stage or session

Estimated Time Length: 30 minutes or less

Materials:
- ✓ A piece of paper shaped to look like a heart
- ✓ Masking or clear tape
- ✓ A marker (which can effectively write over pieces of tape)
- ✓ A brief vignette about a hypothetical child who is experiencing a stressful day at home and at school, or some circumstance which is likely to lead to feelings of sadness and frustration

Activity:
The Torn Heart Treatment Team is an adaptation of the exercise known as *The Torn Heart* as part of the intervention program known as *Don't Laugh at Me* (Roerden, 2000). Group members' names are written on mended pieces of a paper heart. The activity contributes to group cohesiveness, as members choose to commit to helping each other when they come to school feeling sad or frustrated.

Specific Directions for Activity:
Gather the group members together and briefly call attention to the fact that sometimes people have difficult days and that it can affect how they approach other people and also how they view themselves. Mention that one of the more significant things that can be impacted by these difficulties is the heart.
- ✓ There are times in life when things don't always go our way, or we feel and think things that bring us down. Sometimes these things happen at school, at home, in our neighborhood, or all over the place. When these things happen to some people, they feel it in their heart: like this one (hold up the paper heart).
- ✓ Now I am going to tell you a story about someone who is having one of these hard times. Pay attention to me as I read the story, and show you how it impacts this person's heart.

The leader then tells the story, and after each sentence that relates to a moment of frustration or sadness that the main character of the story experiences, the leader rips into the heart.

John was late getting up for school today because he didn't hear his alarm clock go off (rip the heart slightly). He saw he had only a few minutes to get dressed, eat, and catch the school bus. He didn't have time to shower (rip the heart slightly). His parents had already left for work, and didn't leave him any breakfast (rip the heart). He tried very hard to get dressed and leave the house on time, but ended up missing the bus (rip the heart).

He ended up having to walk all the way to school on his own, and he arrived late (rip the heart). He also recognized that he forgot his homework, because he was in such a hurry (rip the heart). He went into school, recognizing that things weren't going so well for him, and while walking down the hall, some kids were making fun of the way he looked and the fact that he was late (rip). He entered the classroom and sat down, not knowing what would happen next."

After the story is completed, and the torn mass of the paper heart is shown to the group, the leader asks the group members to state how the child within the story may be feeling as a result of the circumstances (s)he has experienced. After hearing the responses of the group members to the previous question, ask them if they have ever felt the way that the story's character has.

Members give feeling-based answers at this time. After answering this question, the leader asks the group members to come up with some ideas as to how this student can be helped out by people like them.

As members provide responses to this question, the leader takes pieces of tape and puts them over the ripped pieces of the heart. Each piece of tape symbolizes a way in which some kind of strategy and/or solution can be given to someone in order to work through sad or frustrating feelings. The leader also writes the name of the member who came up with a particular answer over the piece of tape in a dark ink, with the expectation that all members at some point will be able to provide an answer.

Hold up the taped (or "treated" heart) and show the group members how they worked as a team to produce this new heart. Ask the group members what they think the lesson behind the exercise is, and use this as a moment to close the group.

Processing Questions/Conclusion:
 ✓ How do you think the story's character (John, in this case) is feeling right now?
 ✓ What might happen to John if something else does not go his way?
 ✓ What are some things that you/we can do to help John work through these feelings?
 ✓ How do these things that you/we have come up with relate to what you/we can do for others at school, in this group, and elsewhere?

Cautions:
The leader needs to be sure that all members are included in the mending of the heart. The purpose of this version of the exercise is not only to show members that they can individually come up with strategies to work through negative feelings and situations, but also that they can do it as a team. Members who feel excluded or do not participate may not be able to recognize this point and therefore, may not attain this goal.

The leader also needs to be careful not to only focus on each member's personal problems when asking if anyone has ever felt the way that the story's character has. Members who over-personalize the exercise may also not aid in the group's ability to reach the exercise's ultimate goals.

Credit/References:
Roerden, L. P. (2000). *Don't laugh at me. Teacher's guide: Grades 6-8. Creating a ridicule-free classroom.* New York: Educators for Social Responsibility.

About the Group Worker:
Adam P. Zagelbaum, Ph.D., NCC is an Assistant Professor in the Counseling Program at Sonoma State University with primary teaching responsibilities in School Counseling.

For Girls Only

Submitted by Nikki S. Currie

Goals:
- ✓ Celebrate inner and outer beauty
- ✓ Gain information on daily life skills, healthy living habits

Target population: Girls ages 11-15

Potential Stage/Session(s): Transition or working stage

Estimated Time Length: Two hours

Materials: Community volunteer/presenter typically provides materials

Activity:
This activity uses a community presenter to provide information and skills on personal health and beauty. The community presenter may provide information on healthy eating and exercise routines, hairstyles and hair care, or skin care and make-up. Typically, this activity is set within a context of a group curriculum focusing on specific topic of interest to adolescent females. However, the activity may be adapted for use in other contexts.

Specific Directions for Activity:
Group is opened with an activity entitled *My Name*. Each participant writes her name vertically on a piece of paper she is given. Each participant writes a word that starts with the letter of her name out to the side that describes who she is as a person.

An example follows:

S – smiley	K - kind
A – adventurous	A - active
L – likeable	R - responsible
L – loving	A - animated
Y – young	

Each participant is invited to share her name and words to describe her to the group. The counselor introduces the concept of inner beauty. Some questions to facilitate the discussion might be:
- ✓ What is inner beauty?
- ✓ What are some inward characteristics that you view as beautiful either in yourself or others?
- ✓ How is inward and outward beauty related?

In the second portion of the group, the counselor introduces the community presenter. As an example, a beauty consultant may serve as the community presenter. The beauty consultant gives each participant a make-up tray with cleanser, cotton balls, astringent, and moisturizer on it. She instructs the girls how to cleanse their face with cleanser and gives each a warm wet washcloth to wipe off the cleanser. Next she explains how to apply astringent and moisturizer. She emphasizes the importance of daily skin care, healthy eating, living, and sleep habits and how these also contribute to beautiful skin. Next, she gives each girl a sample packet of make-up and places a circle of foundation in each makeup tray. She explains how to apply a foundation, and items in the sample packet (blush, eye shadow, lip liner, lip gloss, and mascara. Finally, she discusses with the girls the importance of applying minimal make-up to let natural beauty shine through. The beauty consultant then answers any questions the girls might have.

Processing Questions/Conclusion:
- ✓ What part of the session did you enjoy the most?
- ✓ What part of the session did you enjoy the least?
- ✓ What information was the most beneficial to you?
- ✓ What information was the least beneficial to you?
- ✓ Do girls and women have to wear make-up to be beautiful?
- ✓ Using make-up is just one way of choosing to celebrate your outer beauty. What are some others?
- ✓ What is one thing you will do this week to celebrate your beauty?

Cautions:
Be sure to remind the community presenter one week prior to their session.

About the Group Worker:
Nikki S. Currie, MS, LPC, NCC, is presently a faculty member in the Department of Counseling, Educational, and School Psychology at Wichita State University in Wichita, Kansas and a doctoral student at Kansas State University in Manhattan, Kansas.

A Garden as a Metaphor for Change in Group
Submitted by Janice L. DeLucia-Waack

Goals:
✓ Explore individual goals for the group
✓ Identify obstacles to change and adjust the atmosphere to enhance group experience

Target population: Ages 12-18
Must be able to grasp a metaphor

Potential Stage/Session(s): Orientation: Second or third session

Estimated Time Length: Can be 20 minutes to two sessions (does need some prep time during or before the session)

Materials: Chalkboard or wall to hang images, tape, pictures of flowers, weeds, shovels, rocks, and watering cans

Activity:
Reading of Metaphor: Begin by reading the *Pulling Weeds and Planting Flowers Story* (Anderson, 1994)

> Let's imagine it is a nice spring day and you want to start a garden. You go out and see that there are a lot of weeds. You put on your old comfortable clothes, get on some gardening gloves, kneel down, and start pulling out those weeds. Soon all those weeds are gone and you feel pleasantly tired but proud about what you've done. There's that old garden free of weeds, with the good dirt clearly visible again. So you take off your gloves, walk into the house, sit down, and tell yourself what a nice garden you have.

> What's wrong with this picture? Of course, you say, you have to plant some flowers! Well, effective psychotherapy is more than pulling up weeds, and trying to get rid of the rocks and twigs that are covering up good earth. It means planting flowers, not just pulling up weeds. The whole purpose of removing your self-defeating patterns of behavior, recognizing what hasn't worked well, is to start cultivating thoughts and behaviors that produce "flowers." Getting rid of the problem areas is only the first step to growth and development. The real purpose of psychotherapy is to help you get on with your life, to produce something good and worthwhile, to grow flowers and fruit. Effective gardening does not stop after pulling out weeds.

Specific Directions for Activity:
After reading the *Pulling Weeds and Planting Flowers* story, facilitate reflection on the metaphor and its application to group

Questions:
- ✓ What do you think the message is?
- ✓ How is this a metaphor for how our group works?
- ✓ What are the weeds? Flowers? Stones? Watering cans? Shovels?

Emphasize that good habits (flowers) must be planted to replace bad habits (weeds) so group helps stop doing things that are not helpful and also teaches (grows) new ways of thinking, feeling, and behaving that are productive and helpful.

Dyad Activity:
Then ask group members to choose a partner to discuss how they will work in group with. Pass out 2 flowers, weeds, rocks, and watering cans to each group member. Give them between 8 and 20 minutes to write down and discuss with a partner:
- ✓ Their goal(s) (what they want to learn) as the flower to plant
- ✓ Their weed as the negative behavior or attitude to get rid of
- ✓ Rocks that get in the way of planting new flowers
- ✓ Watering can as the things they need from group to help them grow

Group Sharing of Weeds and Flower:
Ask members to respond to the following questions.
- ✓ The watering cans? What will they contribute uniquely to group?
- ✓ The flowers? What behaviors/skills/thoughts do they want to develop?
- ✓ The weeds? What behaviors/thoughts/feelings do they want to stop doing?
- ✓ The stones? What gets in the way of change?
- ✓ What shovels do you need to use?
- ✓ How will we work together as gardeners?

Ask group members to hang up their pictures on the board after they share them. All group members should be encouraged to share at least one flower and one watering can, emphasizing the positives for the group. Start with the positive to encourage cohesion.

Processing Questions/Conclusion:
Ask group members to reflect on the following questions.
- ✓ Similarities in flowers to plant?
- ✓ Weeds to weed? Stones?
- ✓ How will they work together as a group to plant these flowers? Pull up weeds? Turn over the stones into a fence?
- ✓ What watering cans will be useful?
- ✓ How will you ask for that help?
- ✓ Whose watering can do you want to borrow sometime?
- ✓ What will each of you bring to the group that can help the group as a whole or another group member?
- ✓ What was it like to talk with someone about this?
- ✓ Was it easier to share 1st with one person, then notice similarities, then share as a large group?

Instruct group members at any point to approach the board and pull out a weed or move a rock or move the flower up as they learn things…. "Let's move the rocks into a wall, something useful."

Cautions:
It is helpful to ask group members to think about what they want to learn, positive and negative, before group so they put thought into it.

Sometimes people will not want to share their weeds (and or will share them but not want to hang them up). This is okay; let students keep them and sometimes later in group they will share.
It is helpful to give examples of each (my flower is wanting to be more realistic about myself, my weed is that I want to be liked by everyone, my stone is that peer pressure; I do what others want me to, etc.)

Credit/References:
Anderson, A. (1994). Stories I'd tell my patients: Pulling weeds and
    planting flowers. *Eating Disorders: The Journal of Treatment and Prevention, 2,*
    184-185.

I first learned about the metaphor from Dr. Cyndee Kalodner who used it with eating disorder clients. I then used it with my groups course who took off with it, adding the pictures.

About the Group Worker:
Dr. Janice L. DeLucia-Waack is an Associate Professor in the Department of Counseling, School, and Educational Psychology at the University at Buffalo, SUNY, a former editor of the *Journal for Specialists in Group Work*, former ASGW President, and Fellow in the Association for Specialists in Group Work.

Staying Safe Online
Submitted by Kelly Duncan and Holly Nikels

Goals:
  ✓ Inform middle school students about safe online practices
  ✓ Explore and reinforce reasons why personal safety is important

Target population: Ages 11-14

Potential Stage/Session(s): Any stage or session

Estimated Time Length: 45 minutes

Materials: *Rules for Online Safety* handout

Activity:
In this psychoeducational activity, students identify strategies for safe internet use. A handout is used to help illustrate specific online dangers and strategies for avoiding online dangers, including online predators. Students are then challenged to apply these principles to their own online practices.

First, introduce the topic. Describe potentially dangerous situations to students and provide the *Rules for Online Safety* handout. Ask students, have they ever felt uncomfortable with online material? Have there been situations where they wondered if they were safe, or have they heard of others who have been harmed. by unsafe online practices? After discussing the relevance of the topic, proceed to additional processing questions.

Processing Questions/Conclusion:

  ✓ Why is it important to understand being safe while using the internet?
  ✓ What are some of the dangers for individuals using the internet? How can you avoid these dangers?
  ✓ What should you do if you are contacted by a stranger online?
  ✓ What should you do if you are bullied by someone while online?
  ✓ How could you share this information with your parents or other important adults in your life?

About the Group Workers:
Dr. Kelly Duncan is a former School Counselor and is currently an Assistant Professor in the Department of Counseling at the University of South Dakota in Vermillion, where she serves as the School Counseling Program Coordinator.

Holly Nikels is an Associate Professor in the Department of Counselor Education at Western Illinois University. Prior to becoming a Counselor Educator she worked in school and community counseling positions.

Rules for Online Safety

1. I will not give out personal information such as my address, telephone number, parents' work address/telephone number, or the name and location of my school without my parents' permission.

2. I will tell my parents right away if I come across any information that makes me feel uncomfortable.

3. I will never agree to get together with someone I "meet" online without first checking with my parents. If my parents agree to the meeting, I will be sure that it is in a public place and bring my mother or father along.

4. I will never send a person my picture or anything else without first checking with my parents.

5. I will not respond to any messages that are mean or in any way make me feel uncomfortable. It is not my fault if I get a message like that. If I do I will tell my parents right away so that they can contact the service provider.

6. I will talk with my parents so that we can set up rules for going online. We will decide upon the time of day that I can be online, the length of time I can be online and appropriate areas for me to visit. I will not access other areas or break these rules without their permission.

7. I will not give out my Internet password to anyone (even my best friends) other than my parents.

8. I will check with my parents before downloading or installing software or doing anything that could possibly hurt our computer or jeopardize my family's privacy

9. I will be a good online citizen and not do anything that hurts other people or is against the law.

10. I will help my parents understand how to have fun and learn things online and teach them things about the Internet, computers and other technology.

Rules one through six are adapted from the brochure <u>Child Safety on the Information Highway</u> by SafeKids.Com founder Larry Magid. (© 2004 National Center for Missing and Exploited Children). Rules 7 through 10 are copyrighted by Larry Magid (© 2005)

Personal Boundaries:
Doors to My Heart

Submitted by Louisa L. Foss and Maria Foss Rand

Goals:
- ✓ Gain basic understanding of the importance of healthy interpersonal boundaries
- ✓ Identify one's own interpersonal boundary style in different situations
- ✓ Increase empowerment in coping with negative interpersonal influences

Target population: Ages 14-18
May be tailored for use depending on larger group goals (i.e., used in the context of a healthy dating relationships group or healthy friendships group).

Potential Stage/Session(s): Working stage

Estimated Time Length: 45 minutes

Materials: Blank paper and drawing pencils or makers

Activity:
This activity uses the metaphor of a door to describe one's interpersonal boundary style in a variety of situations. Psychoeducation about the importance of healthy boundaries is provided, and students choose what type 'door' they might wish to use with specific relationships. Students are then challenged to identify negative or problematic peer relationships or situations and identify and apply healthy boundary behaviors.

Specific Directions for Activity:
The school counselor introduces the activity be describing interpersonal boundaries. For example, one might say that boundaries are invisible barriers that mark the point at which one person ends and another person begins. We allow others' influences, ideas, and energy to enter our world through our invisible boundaries.

Explain to students that in many ways, boundaries are like doors to our heart. We may allow good influences, ideas, and energy in, or we may keep bad influences, ideas, and energy out. In this way, we can determine who we want to allow in, and who we want to keep out. Ultimately, it is our choice how we wish to interact with others. Note that this abstract concept is often difficult for students to grasp. While explaining the concept to students, be sure to ask questions to check learning and provide clarification and examples as needed.

Explain that the metaphor of a door or gate can be used to describe our boundaries. There are many kinds of doors available. Invite students to list as many as you can. Students can either list these on paper or the counselor can facilitate the discussion with the use of a white board. Some examples of doors might be:
- ✓ Screen door
- ✓ Door with many windows

- ✓ Curtain door
- ✓ Dutch door
- ✓ Padlocked, steel door
- ✓ Pocket door

Facilitate a discussion around all the doors brainstormed by students. For example, a screen door may be used to keep negative influences, ideas, or energy out, while also allowing some freedom to connect with others. For some relationships, one may wish to use a padlocked door. For other relationships, one might want a pocket door which may be invisible to others but used in a hurry to protect oneself from negativity.

Pass out blank pieces of paper. Invite students to list important people in their lives (i.e., parents or other family members, dating partner, important adults, friends, siblings, neighbors). Invite students to select five of the individuals listed and draw the doors or boundaries they use with those individuals. Ask students to share their drawings with the group.

Processing Questions/Conclusion:

- ✓ How are the doors or boundaries on your sheet similar or different from each other?
- ✓ How are the doors or boundaries on your sheet similar or different from other group members' boundaries?
- ✓ Why did you select the individuals you did?
- ✓ Which people on your list do you want to have different boundaries with?
  - o Why?
  - o What might will you do differently that would demonstrate a different kind of boundary?
  - o How will you feel different when you're using that new boundary?
- ✓ Name one thing you plan to do differently in at least one relationship because of what you learned today.

End group by reminding students that they can always choose how they interact with important others. Planning and being proactive to guard one's personal boundaries will help students cope with interpersonal conflict, negative peer influence, or a variety of other difficult interpersonal situations.

About the Group Workers:
Dr. Louisa Foss, PCC (Ohio), NCC, is an Assistant Professor in the Counseling and School Psychology program at Southern Connecticut State University in New Haven, Connecticut.

Maria Foss Rand has a master's degree in Public Administration from the University of Hartford and is a master's student in the Counseling and School Psychology program at Southern Connecticut State University in New Haven, Connecticut.

Writing Your Own Eulogy

Submitted by Amy Poole and Paula T. McWhirter

Goals:
- ✓ Identify future goals
- ✓ Evaluate how current decisions may or may not support future goals

Target population: Ages 15-18

Potential Stage/Session(s): Working stage

Estimated Time Length: Two group sessions of 30-45 minutes each

Materials: Previously completed activities that focus on life experiences, goals for the future and fundamental values; Pen/pencil and paper

Activity: Students are asked to write their own eulogy that describes how they would like to be remembered after they have died. While this may seem like a sober topic, it will provide an opportunity for students to reflect on what they consider their most important values and goals for the future. This kind of activity allows students to reflect on their ideals and dreams and determine whether or not their current behaviors are contributing to or distracting from their ideals and values.

Specific Directions for Activity:
The activity may be introduced with the following:
Over the next two days (sessions) we will be focusing on what you'd like to achieve, accomplish, and be remembered for in your life. You will use the activities we've completed so far (Name Activities) to help you in this activity.
You will have the next few minutes to use the activities you completed earlier (The teacher will need to identify activities done previously that helped students prepare for this activity, such as a lifeline, brainstorming, an outline, or any other activity used to prepare students for this reflective activity) to compose a eulogy that you would like to be read at your funeral.

According to Miriam-Webster, a eulogy is "a speech in praise of someone, especially in honor of one deceased." Although, you are far from your funeral, this activity will give you a chance to reflect upon your life's goals and current direction in life. For the purpose of this activity, your eulogy MUST include the following:
- ✓ Who will deliver the eulogy
- ✓ The age at which you died
- ✓ Any careers you had in your adult life
- ✓ Any leisure activities that were important you
- ✓ Any achievements you would like remembered (this can include your family members, church or civic activities, professional accomplishments, etc.)
- ✓ Some way for the eulogizer to describe you that summarizes your life and how you would like to be remembered
- ✓ This can be in the form of any of the following:
  - o A quote

- o A song
- o A poem
- o An anecdote or experience the eulogizer remembers sharing with you
- o A collection of quotes from people who knew you
- o Any other way that you feel would describe your life experience

Processing Questions/Conclusion:
After the students have finished writing their eulogy, ask them to read over it and circle any part(s) of it that they feel reflect their core values. For example one student's profession as a carpenter may reflect the value they place on being able to work with their hands and be creative. Another example may be their heritage (children and grandchildren) reflecting the importance of family over work. The students should then list at least three values they feel are reflected in their eulogy. Remind students that values are broader than achievements and the way they choose to be remembered (song, poem, anecdote) may be the richest source for identifying their values.

After group members have identified the values they support as most important, ask them to evaluate how they feel those values or ideals are reflected in their current scholastic or extra-curricular activities, or in their current relationships. Ask them to write about each value and discuss how it is or is not currently reflected in their life.

Encourage group members to consider any discrepancies between their lives and values and ask them what is keeping them from incorporating the values in their life.

The reflection on values and current life can be done privately in writing, but ideally would be done in a group setting where the students could share their eulogies, values, and self-assessment. If the group has achieved a sense of cohesiveness through other activities, this discussion could be beneficial both as students reflect on their own actions and receive feedback from other group members.

Cautions:
This activity may not be appropriate for students who have suffered the death of a family member or close friend. Some students may find contemplating their own deaths overwhelming or anxiety provoking and care should be taken to make sure that students vulnerable to being adversely affected by this activity be given the choice to participate or be excluded from this portion of the group process. Additionally, because this topic deals with death, the group leader should be prepared to deal with unexpected reactions as students contemplate their own deaths.

Credit/References:
The initial activity involved adolescents in group therapy for drug and alcohol abuse. This first version involved the creation of two versions of obituaries: one if they continue to use drugs and/or alcohol and another if they remain or obtain sobriety. This original activity was presented by Dee Rentie, a counselor at the Moore Youth and Family Services to students at the Moore Alternative School and Treatment program. In addition, the life-planning approach used in the current activity proposal uses ideas presented in by Vernon Zunker (2006).

Eulogy. In *Merriam-Webster's collegiate dictionary* (p. 368, 11ᵗʰ ed.). (2001). Springfield,
    MA: Merriam-Webster.
Zunker, V. G. (2006). *Career counseling: A holistic approach* (7 ed.). Belmont, CA:
    Thompson.

About the Group Workers:
Amy Poole has master's of education in Community Counseling. She currently teaches
for Keystone National High School, an internet-based school.

Paula T. McWhirter, Ph.D., is an Assistant Professor of Counseling Psychology at the
University of Oklahoma.

To Walk in Another's Shoes
Submitted by Jolie Ziomek-Daigle and Anneliese A. Singh

Goals:
- ✓ Define and recognize the diversity in the group and in the school
- ✓ Begin to understand diversity in its many shapes and forms
- ✓ Create and maintain a welcoming and celebratory classroom and school environment for diverse students
- ✓ Impart knowledge and awareness related to marginalized populations

Target Population: Ages 11-18

Potential Stage/Session(s): Any stage or session

Estimated Time Length: 50 minutes (or a class period)

Materials: Paper plates, string/yarn/ribbon, and markers (Optional: magazine cutouts of children/adolescents from diverse backgrounds)

Activity: This small group focuses on community building and increasing cultural awareness. In this activity, "people plates" representing diverse individuals are created and worn to increase cultural awareness among group members. Through becoming an individual from a diverse background, group members come to explore, values, and celebrate many aspects of diversity.

Specific Directions for Activity:
This activity includes six steps:
- ✓ Welcoming all the students to the activity and establish group rules regarding respect, taking turns to talk, etc.
- ✓ Becoming aware of diversity around the room in its many shapes and forms
- ✓ Trying on a "hat" of an individual from a diverse background (gender, race, ethnicity, sexual orientation, religion, disability, age) to better understand historical and sociopolitical influences
- ✓ Coming together as a community and sharing their experiences
- ✓ Address the intersections of diversity (gender, race, ethnicity, sexual orientation, religion, disability, age) and how each individual brings something unique to the group
- ✓ Identify strengths of individuals and how to use those strengths for one's own self.

Pregroup Preparation
First, make people plates. On a paper plate, write or paste a typewritten brief biography of an individual from a diverse background (see description below). You may also use magazine cut outs of individuals to complement the biography. Next, use a hole puncher and thread yarn or ribbon so participants can wear the people plate around their necks, laid on their chest. Create enough for the small group or class. Or, make a few and create a fishbowl (group within a group).

Activity Instructions

✓ Following a group introduction and check-in, ask participants to define diversity and what diversity means to them. Sample questions include:
  - How are they diverse as a group?
  - How have they learned from the diversity that the school/community brings?
  - How does each person bring a unique piece of diversity? But, what are also the commonalities of the group?

✓ Provide a people plate for each participant. Or, select/ask volunteers to participate in a fish bowl activity. For each "people plate," prepare a description of a diverse individual.

Examples of people plates:

✓ "Hi, my name is Pilar and I am in 10ᵗʰ grade. I was born in Columbia and came to the Unites States with my parents when I was 4. I am the only person in my immediate family that speaks fluent English so I must communicate for my parents. We have lived with various family members throughout my life as my dad has a hard time keeping jobs. My parents often have difficulty coming to my school because of working and transportation. I earn B's and want to go to a college where I can make friends like me."

✓ "Hi, my name is Lane. I am Jewish, white and both my parents work. When I was younger, I had a crush on another boy. I thought this was wrong until my teacher said that lots of people are attracted to individuals of the same sex. Now that I am in high school, I have found friends like me and that makes me feel safe. I want to go to a college or find a job after high school where I can be myself."

✓ "Hi, my name is Saundra. I am an African-American with cerebral palsy. I am in 7ᵗʰ grade and often take classes with other students like me. I enjoy those classes but also like being with "regular" students who are different than me. I am awful at Math and regularly attend tutoring. I have a lot of friends but sometimes I hear people making fun of me in the lunchroom or on the playground. I often wonder what kind of job I will have after graduation because of my disability and my parents don't have a lot of money. I worry a lot about that. My school counselor says that there is an agency in my neighborhood that might help me with those decisions. I am going to check it out."

Processing Questions/Conclusion:

Discuss the unique aspects the individual brings to the group/class/community.

✓ How do the many pieces of the person intersect?
✓ How have those pieces been oppressed throughout history?
✓ How are those pieces being oppressed in our class, school, community, right now?
✓ What can we do as a school/community to make everyone feel welcomed. and celebrated?

Identify strengths of the diverse individual.
- ✓ What strengths did the person possess?
- ✓ What were the person's hopes and dreams?
- ✓ Can you identify with one or more pieces of that person? If so, what?
- ✓ How can you use that piece to grow a piece of yourself to be a stronger and more fulfilled individual?

Cautions:
The group worker needs to view diversity as broadly defined and allow the students to include many forms of diversity (age, gender, race, ethnicity, family make up, religion, SES, disability, sexual orientation). The workers must also be aware of any personal biases towards marginalized populations. Developmental considerations must be addressed. For example, language on the people plate describing individuals from diverse backgrounds may need to be less complex for middle school students.

About the Group Workers:
Dr. Ziomek-Daigle , LPC, RPT-S, is a former School Counselor with New Orleans Public Schools and a current faculty member at The University of Georgia.

Dr. Singh is on the editorial board of the *Journal for Specialists in Group Work* and her group practice experiences include design, implementation, and evaluation of LGBT youth groups in high school, college, and community settings.

Activities
for All Ages

Feeling 4-Square
Submitted by Melissa Luke

Goals: To teach and expand an affective vocabulary. Specifically, students explore the similarities and differences between various feelings, using examples from both a shared reading and their own experiences to differentiate between the affective states.

Target Population: All ages

Potential Stage/Session(s): Orientation or transition stage

Estimated Time Length: Completion may require two separate 30-45 minute sessions

Materials: The school counselor intentionally selects a shared reading that contains examples of a variety of feelings. The reading will elicit discussion beyond the material in the text; however the content of the shared reading will launch the group's focus.

- ✓ Depending upon the age of student participants, the group worker(s) either brings in a book to read aloud or makes copies of the material for each group member.
- ✓ Ideally, four large sheets of poster board are used to construct the Feeling 4-Square. It is also possible to simply divide a white board into 4 equal sections. The 4 sections are labeled as follows: Mad, Sad, Glad, Afraid.
- ✓ Prior to the group session, the group worker(s) use the shared reading as a stimulus to generate a list of affective states, but additional ideas are also included. These words are then written on 'Feeling cards,' with one word per card. Index cards (3x5) work well for this, but slips of paper are equally effective. Generally a 4-5 'Feeling cards' per group member ratio provides enough material for effective processing.
- ✓ Once the cards are made, they are shuffled and placed into a container from which students will pick (e.g., hat, large envelope, bowl).
- ✓ Adhesive tape is required so that students can adhere the feeling cards in the appropriate quadrant of the Feeling 4-Square.

Activity: This activity uses a story with affective elements to demonstrate and apply feelings identification among the students. The four main types of feelings (mad, glad, sad, and afraid) are indicated on each student's Feeling 4-Square (see above). Students identify, explain, and process feelings associated with the story and as they have experienced them in their own lives.

Specific Directions for Activity:
Depending upon the reading abilities of the group members, either the school counselor reads the shared reading or asks for a volunteer(s) to do so.

Following the reading, the school counselor processes the content of the reading and leads a discussion about the affect that was experienced within the story, as well as in group members in reaction to the reading.

The students are invited to share other possible feeling responses to the events. After this discussion, the school counselor introduces the Feeling 4-Square, saying that although there are infinite 'feelings,' most can be boiled down to 4 main types (The counselor may want to be clear that this is one possible view.)

The school counselor invites students to suggest their thoughts about what these may be, and then reveal the categories of Mad, Glad, Sad, and Afraid.

- ✓ The counselor explains that everyone will have an opportunity to select a feeling card (related to the shared reading), read the feeling out loud, share a personal story or example dealing with a time when they experienced this affect, and then place it in one of the 4 quadrants on the Feeling 4-Square. The school counselor may want to demonstrate this process.
    - o For example, a student may select a feeling card labeled 'frustrated.' She or he would read this word out loud to the group, and then offer a personal example such as 'Earlier today I felt frustrated when my little sister spilled her juice because it got on my favorite jeans and I had to change which made me miss the bus!' Then the student is prompted to place the feeling card in one of the 4 quadrants: Mad, Sad, Glad, or Afraid. She or he then tapes the card to 'Mad.'
    - o The school counselor then invites discussion and reaction.

This process continues until all of the feeling cards are placed and/or the near the session's end. Be sure to allow time for processing.

Processing Questions/Conclusion:
The school counselor summarizes the themes that were presented during the group discussion. The school counselor explains that the experience of feelings is universal, but that there are also many variations.

The following questions can be used in response to the shared reading:
- ✓ How do you think this character felt when X happened?
- ✓ What might be going on for this character right now?
- ✓ What indication do you have about how this character feels?
- ✓ How else might this character be feeling?
- ✓ What other ways might someone respond?
- ✓ If the 'volume' of this feeling was turned up, what would it be?
- ✓ What other feelings are similar to this?
- ✓ What might be the opposite of this feeling?

The following questions can be used in response to students' selection of the feeling card, sharing their story, and placing the card in the Felling 4-Square:
- ✓ How else might someone have felt in this circumstance?
- ✓ What are the similarities between this and what X shared?
- ✓ When have others felt like this?
- ✓ How might you have responded to this feeling?
- ✓ What other ways do people show this feeling?
- ✓ How else might you express this same feeling?
- ✓ What other feeling could be felt in response to this feeling?

Cautions:
It is advised that the counselor determine the level of safety and trust prior to selecting the shared reading. While this activity can facilitate group cohesion and a sense of universality, a basic trust level is necessary in order for students to meaningfully share their experiences.

Additional Comments:
In some instances, when working with older students, the school counselor can invite students to generate the list of affective states and contribute their own ideas as they make the 'feeling cards.'

About the Group Worker:
Melissa Luke, Ph.D., LMHC, NCC, is a former School Counselor and currently works as an Assistant Professor and Coordinator of School Counseling in the Counseling and Human Services department at Syracuse University.

Coping Skills Links
Submitted by Jacqueline M. Swank and Kara P. Ieva

Goals:
- ✓ Distinguish between healthy and unhealthy coping skills
- ✓ Create a list of useable healthy coping skills

Target Population: All ages

Potential Stage/Session(s): Transition or working stage; Used with anger management program after sources, triggers, and targets have been discussed in the group.

Estimated Time Length: 30-45 minutes

Materials:
- ✓ Colored paper
- ✓ Markers, crayons, pens
- ✓ Scissors, tape, stapler
- ✓ Chain links

Activity:
This activity uses the metaphor of a chain to illustrate the importance of using coping skills, specifically for responding to anger in healthy ways. An art activity helps to identify and reinforce the benefit of actively using coping skills.

Specific Directions for Activity:
To introduce the activity to the group, the counselor may talk about a chain having many links designed for a unified purpose. This metaphor is related to using a chain of coping skills for coping with anger in healthy ways.

- ✓ Show the group a link of chains.
- ✓ Ask, "What is a chain used for? How do the links work together?"
- ✓ Discuss unhealthy and healthy coping skills. Discuss how unhealthy coping skills hurt oneself, others, or property and how healthy coping skills do not result in these actions.
- ✓ Explain to children that they will create their own list of healthy coping skills that they will be able to make into a paper chain.

- ✓ Give each child a stack of paper strips and have them write a healthy coping skill on each one.
- ✓ Have children take turns reading their coping skills, adding one link to their chain each time they share a coping skill.
- ✓ Allow children to demonstrate their coping skills, if possible.
- ✓ Discuss where to keep the chain of coping skills and the importance of adding to it.

Processing Questions/Conclusion:
The following statements and questions may be used to prompt additional processing and application:

1. Describe your favorite link of the chain (favorite coping skill) and tell when you could use it.
2. Why do you think it's important to have more than one coping skill?
3. What is important about having healthy coping skills?
4. Share with the group which one of your healthy coping skills you will commit to using this week.

Cautions:
Tape can be used to connect the chain links if staples are not allowed, such as an inpatient hospitalization unit.

Additional Comments:
This activity can also be used to focus on self-esteem by having the children list a positive quality about themselves on each chain.

About the Group Workers:
Jacqueline M. Swank, LCSW, RPT, has worked in a variety of treatment settings including residential, inpatient hospitalization, partial hospitalization, and outpatient.

Kara P. Ieva, M.Ed., NCC, NCSC, has been a professional School Counselor in middle school and high school settings for over nine years.

Breathe In, Breathe Out
Submitted by Rachel Vitale

Goals:
- ✓ Understand mind-body connections as illustrated by the relaxing effects of deep breathing
- ✓ Demonstrate knowledge of deep breathing exercises, either in the classroom or in smaller groups

Target Populations: All ages; Tends to work best with students who are clearly voluntary rather than mandated group participants

Potential Stage/Session(s): Transition or working stage

Estimated Time Length: 20-25 minutes

Materials:
- ✓ Music for relaxation (sounds of nature, classical, etc.), mats, towels, or a clean floor.

Activity:
This relaxation experience may be used to illustrate the connection between the body and emotions. Once a basic level of trust is established, group members can effectively use and process this breathing exercise. Group members may be encouraged to engage in breathing or other relaxation techniques outside of group.

Specific Directions for Activity:
Prior to the group session, begin playing relaxing music in the group room. The music should be quietly playing in the background as students arrive to the group.

The group leader facilitates a psychoeducational discussion on the nature of stress. Prompt questions may include the following:
- ✓ What is stress?
- ✓ What causes you stress?
- ✓ Where do you feel stress in your body?
- ✓ How do you act when you are stressed?
- ✓ What are some things you have tried to reduce stress?

Introduce the relaxation activity.
- ✓ Have the students pick up a mat or towel and find a place on the floor where they are not touching other students when they lay down.
- ✓ Invite students to lie on their backs, place their hands on the upper chest and breathe into the upper chest, then slowly exhale.
- ✓ Next have students place their hands on the ribcage and slowly breathe into the ribcage, then slowly exhale.
- ✓ Students then place their hands on their stomachs, allowing for a slow breath in. This time have them hold their breath for a count of five, then slowly exhale.
- ✓ Finally steps B through D should be repeated.

Processing Questions/Conclusion:

After the exercise, have the students slowly get up and return to the circle to process the experience.

- ✓ On a scale of one to ten how stressed did you feel before? How stressed do you feel now?
- ✓ How does your body feel now?
- ✓ Do you think that you would act differently now that you are more relaxed?
- ✓ Is this something you think you could do in class before an exam or if you are starting to feel anxious?
- ✓ What are some other situations where this exercise might help?

Directions: Have students sit in chairs or desks. With their arms resting on the desk or their laps have the students practice the same deep breathing as above.

Cautions:

Make sure that you point out to students that when they practice this exercise at their seats, they are able to engage in deep breathing without drawing excessive attention to themselves. If time, space or comfort levels does not allow for students to lie on the floor, the activity is just as effective when the students remain seated.

About the Group Worker:

Rachel Vitale has a Master's degree in School Counseling and is pursuing her Ph.D. in Counselor Education at Kent State University in Kent, Ohio.

Memory Quilt
Submitted by Debora Beck Smith

Goals:
- ✓ Assist students through the grief process after the death of an immediate family member

Target Population: All ages; Students have lost an immediate family member

Potential Stage/Session(s): Working stage

Estimated Time Length: Depends on size of project, ability of student and counselor. Ex.-4-6 square pictures with 2 rows of border took 2 of us about 10-15 (1/2 hour sessions). Younger students will need adult to do most of the quilting. Quilting can be done by machine by adult if desired.

Materials:
- ✓ 81/2 X11inch white paper (copy)
- ✓ crayons or colored pencils
- ✓ white cotton /polyester blend fabric
- ✓ fabric crayons or markers (I use markers)
- ✓ fabric to frame the picture squares and fabric for backing
- ✓ quilt batting (crib size fits most) thin or light loft (So it is easy to sew through)
- ✓ pins, needles, shears
- ✓ large curved quilting safety pins or regular ones
- ✓ quilting thread and quilt label
- ✓ Permanent fine marker for writing
- ✓ Quilting hoop or frame (these are wooden or plastic)

Activity: This activity allows the student to use their creativity to make a quilt or wall hanging that will help them to remember their loved one.

Specific Directions for Activity:

After a check-in, the counselor introduces the activity. An example of an introduction is as follows:
"We may lose a loved one but we always have them in our heart and in our memories. One way that I have combined my love of sewing with helping a student with the loss of a loved one is through creating a memory quilt or wall hanging. First, we need to look at all the good memories the student has of the person. We also discuss that person's favorite things and sports and hobbies. Anything that will help the student remember this person fondly. Sometimes the student works on these ideas at home with the help of other family members."

<u>Pregroup Preparation</u>
- ✓ Gather all materials needed.
- ✓ Precut white fabric for the drawings.

- ✓ Mark off ½" margins on copy paper.
- ✓ Assemble quilt top by machine.
- ✓ Mark quilting lines with pencil or washable quilt marker.
- ✓ Aim for stitches that are ½" or less.
- ✓ Label the quilt, "In memory of..., designed by and quilted by..." and the date.
- ✓ Include washing directions (Wash in cold water, line dry or dry with low heat.

<u>Activity Instructions</u>

Remind students that part of the grief process is remembering and celebrating the happy memories that were shared with the loved one. Invite students to make a list of good memories of their loved one.

Students may use regular crayons to draw pictures of these memories on the copy paper (Mark off ½" margins on paper for seam allowances later so you do not lose any of the design when you sew). The number of blocks depends upon the student. Most are 4, 6 or 9 blocks. Make sure all paper blocks are placed in the same direction. Landscape view is most helpful.

Students are then invited to share their drawings with the group. Some questions to process this segment of the group include the following:
- ✓ What's the very best memory you have of your loved one?
- ✓ How did you feel while you were drawing about these memories?
- ✓ Was it easy or hard for you to think of good memories?

After sharing and processing, students trace these drawing onto the white fabric that is cut into 8 ½ X 11" blocks. Use fabric crayons or markers for fabric.

- ✓ See directions for heat setting the pictures on package of markers or crayons
- ✓ Counselor cuts fabric for framing of blocks. I use one fabric around the blocks and another around the group of blocks. I like contrasting colors.
- ✓ Assist student in the layout of the blocks. Arrange so they look appealing-color, type of design (balance blocks that have a lot of words among colorful picture blocks)
- ✓ Counselor pins fabric framing around each block and machine sews them together using ½" seam allowances (See a quilt book if you need more help)
- ✓ Attach next fabric around this block of blocks. This is the quilt top
- ✓ Press seam allowances toward framing fabric with iron, cut quilt batting about 2" larger than the quilt top.
- ✓ Cut backing fabric about 3" larger than the quilt top. You can use white or solid fabric or a patterned one. This will show on the front, as it will fold up to become the quilt binding.

✓ Lay these layers out as follows. Backing fabric with right side face down. Then lay batting on top. Lay out quilt top with right side up. Smooth out any wrinkles and center the layers. It will be like a sandwich. Pin together. Students can help you to pin the layers by using large curved quilting safety pins. You can hand baste the layers also by sewing a large cross and X across the quilt to keep the layers from shifting.

Following the group, the remaining quilting work is completed:
✓ Use a large quilting hoop or standing hoop to hold the quilt while you quilt.
✓ If you are new to quilting, a step-by-step book may be purchased at any craft store.
✓ Complete a purchased quilt label with a permanent marker and attach to the back of the quilt.

Processing Questions/Conclusion:
✓ What will you remember about this person?
✓ What kind of activities did you do with this person?
✓ What was their job or career?
✓ What were their favorite foods, colors, sports, hobbies?
✓ Did you take any special family trips together?
✓ What do you plan to do with your quilt?

Additional Comments:
When possible, strips of clothing of the deceased person may be used around the blocks. For example neckties and dress shirts work very well. Other fabrics may be used to reflect the interests of the loved one, such as musical notes, tiger prints, etc.

Warn students that small writing will not be legible. Encourage students to keep writing to a minimum, limited to key words or phrases.

About the Group Worker:
Debora Beck Smith is an elementary School Counselor for Massillon City Schools in northeast Ohio.

Circle of Hands
Submitted by Nikki Currie

Goals:
- ✓ Identify positive and negative aspects of the group
- ✓ Develop positive group norms

Target population: All ages

Potential Stage/Session(s): Orientation stage

Estimated Time Length: 50 minutes

Materials: large poster board, approximately 24" X 24" (depending on the group size); magic markers; pencils; Group Norm handout - one per group member

Activity:
  a. First the group leader welcomes everyone to the group and asks group members to sit on the floor. Then the leader explains briefly what group is (a review from the prescreening interview) and that they are going to set up guidelines for the group.
  b. Next, the leader asks each group member to place his/her hand on the poster board in a circle, with one thumb touching the adjacent person next to him/her.
  c. The group leader would model the following: taking a pencil, the leader would outline the hand of the person to the right of him/her, making sure that thumbs are still touching on the poster, forming a circle.
  d. Each group member would continue around the circle, drawing around the hand of the member to his/her right. (It is also wise to add 1 or 2 additional blank hands in the circle if it is an open group to allow for new members to become part of the circle).
  e. The group leader has each member pick a magic marker and outline their hands, and then write their first name or initials inside the hand outline.
  f. The leader explains to the group that they are going to "brainstorm" and discuss what brainstorming means. Then the leader asks group members what kinds of things would make each member want to come to group, what would make it a good place to come to, in a "go round" fashion. The group facilitator would start by saying "Confidentiality" and discuss this. Each time the leader or member says one thing, the facilitator writes it in the middle of the "Circle of Hands."
  g. The group leader then asks the opposite question as to what would make each member *not* want to come to group, as above.
  h. The next step would be to lead group members in an open discussion concerning the purpose of this activity.

i. The leader would then help the group members take the positive things in the middle of the "Circle of Hands" and reduce them 4 or 5 major categories in developing the group norms. Once the group decides which ones are the most important (Confidentiality being required), those are circled and a discussion follows concerning the guidelines that were selected.

j. The group leader takes each individual guideline and discusses it with the members, asks for examples of what this would "look" and "sound" like to make sure that all members understand each guideline.

k. Finally, the group leader gives each member a piece of paper with "Group Guidelines" typed at the top in large font, and numbered from 1 to 5. Group members would then copy down the group guidelines on the sheet and put it in their own group folders.

Processing Questions/Conclusion:
✓ When I say the word "guidelines" what do you think of?
✓ What does the word brainstorming mean?
✓ Why do you think we drew a circle with hands touching?
✓ What kind of things in group would make it a place that you would want to come to each week?
✓ What kind of things in group would make it a place that you would *not* want to come to each week? What do you notice about the two?
✓ Look in the middle of the circle at the things you felt were important for group. Out of these, we are going to form our guidelines. Let's see if we can put these in groupings. Are there words that go together and fit under a main topic?
✓ Through discussion, narrow guidelines to 4 or 5 and circle with a marker.
✓ Let's take each guideline individually. If I walked in the room right now and you were following this guideline, what would it look like? What would it sound like? Now that we have come up with our guidelines for group, would you please copy them on your handout and put it in your group folder. Each time you come to group, we will go over the guidelines before we start. What reasons do you think we have for reviewing our guidelines each week?

Cautions:
One caution for the activity is to ensure that "Confidentiality" is the first guideline and that this is explained and required for group. Also, if this is an open group, be sure to have left some handprints blank for the addition of new members names.

Credit/References:
The title of the activity was taken from the following reference; however, the activity differs in content and purpose:

Jones, A. (2002). *More team-building activities for every group.* Richland, WA: Rec Room Publishing.

About the Group Worker:
Nikki S. Currie, M.S., LPC, NCC, is presently a faculty member in the Department of Counseling, Educational, and School Psychology at Wichita State University in Wichita, Kansas and a doctoral student at Kansas State University in Manhattan, Kansas.

A Collage of Memories
Submitted by Judy Green

Goals:
- ✓ Provide an opportunity to share memories of a loved one who has died
- ✓ Help group members realize that grief is unique to each person

Target population: All ages

Potential Stage/Session(s): Working stage

Estimated Time Length: 1-2 hours

Materials: Old magazines and/or pictures (or copies of photos), scissors, paste or glue sticks, 11"x14" construction paper or posterboard

Activity:
In this activity, group members have an opportunity to share about their loved one who has died in a supportive environment. Prior to the session, ask group members to find in magazine or bring in pictures of things that remind them of their deceased loved one.

At the beginning of the group, explain that each member will be making a collage of things that remind him/her of someone who has died. Because each person's grief is unique, no two collages will be alike. Explain that many things can remind us of the loved one who has died.

Processing Questions/Conclusion: When all collages are complete, allow each member to share his/her collage by displaying it and telling why each picture was chosen. Other members may also ask questions.

After each member has had a chance to present his/her collage, process with the whole group how it felt to do this activity, including how it felt when asked to do it; how it felt while doing it, and how it felt to share.

Take a few minutes to allow each member to tell what he/she will now do with the collage.

Cautions: Any time you are working with grief issues, you must be aware of how the group members appear to be handling this task. If anyone seems upset by the task, talk privately about what feelings the child may be experiencing. Depending on many factors (relationship to the deceased, type of death, time since the death, etc.), a child may not be ready for this activity. By the working stage of a group, however, the leader will most likely know if this activity might cause distress.

About the Group Worker:
Dr. Judy Green, LPCC, is a retired School Counselor and currently is an Associate Professor and School Counseling Coordinator in Counseling and Human Development at Walsh University, North Canton, Ohio.

Termination Capsule
Submitted by Melissa Luke

Goals:
- ✓ Improve interpersonal communication
- ✓ Facilitate delivery and receipt of interpersonal feedback
- ✓ Consolidate group members' experiences of group counseling
- ✓ Effectively close the group

Target Population: All ages

Potential Stage/Session(s): Termination stage/ Second to last session

Estimated Time Length: Approximately 40 minutes

Materials: Each capsule is made from two clear soft drink bottles. Therefore, two bottles are needed for each group member. Additionally, colored index cards provide an excellent medium for group members to record their answers to the prompts. However, construction or copy paper divided into quarters also works well. Colored markers or other writing utensils are needed for each group member as well.

Activity:
This group activity draws upon narrative theory in assisting students in consolidating their experiences of group counseling. During the activity, students are prompted to reflect upon and write their thoughts, feelings, and reactions about a variety of experiences within the group. The counselor provides a series of 8-12 prompts for this purpose.

Additionally, group members also communicate interpersonal reactions and feedback to one another. All group members have the opportunity to share the components of their 'Termination Capsule' through a read aloud, and are encouraged to talk about any of their experiences within the activity itself.

Specific Directions for Activity:
To introduce this activity, counselors will have previously discussed the ending of the group, and processed some of the mixed reactions that often accompany such. Moreover, the counselors will inform the group that the activity has two main goals: to honor and memorialize each group member's unique experience in the group and to facilitate their reflection and interpersonal communication about their experiences.

School counselors may want to make the capsules prior to the group, or they can also do so with the group members. To make the capsules, the labels are removed from the bottles and they are rinsed and dried. Next, the necks of the bottles are cut off both bottles, leaving 2 cylinder shaped vessels. A slit is made in one of the vessels, beginning at the open edge and continuing 2/3 of the way down. This will enable this half of the capsule to slide inside the other half.

Steps in the activity:
1. Each group member is given a capsule (made of two soft drink bottles). Stacks of colored paper and markers are provided, so that group members can select from these as they construct their 'Termination Capsule.'
2. Counselors explain that this activity is designed to help group members record their important thoughts, feelings, and experiences from group, much like a time capsule that is buried in a building foundation to document important aspects of the time period in which the building is constructed. However, because they will take their 'Termination Capsule with them (and it will not be buried), they will be able to refer back to it any time they want.
3. The counselors explain that they will ask each group member a series of questions about their experiences in group and that each group member will select a piece of paper to record their answer. Once they have done this, they are asked to fold the paper and place it inside their 'Termination Capsule.' The last two prompts involve group members offering their thoughts about and hopes for one another. Therefore, they give each other the folded paper as contributions to one another's 'Termination Capsule.'

Examples of potential questions that can be used as prompts within the activity are as follows:
  ✓ What is something important that you will take from your experience of this group?
  ✓ What did you learn about yourself in this group? What did you learn about others?
  ✓ What is one way in which you are similar to others in this group and one way in which you are unique?
  ✓ What remains unsaid in this group? What keeps it unsaid?
  ✓ How will you continue what has been started in this group?
  ✓ List two resources (people, places, things) to which you could refer to in the future if needed.
  ✓ Discuss an example of a powerful emotion that you experienced in the group.
  ✓ Describe a time when you applied something that you learned in the group to a situation outside of the group.
  ✓ Explain one way in which your thinking has changed related to what you have experienced in the group.
  ✓ What is a wish/ hope/goal that you have for yourself in the future?
  ✓ What is a wish/ hope/goal that you have for each of your group members?
  ✓ What is one fond thing that you will remember about each group member?

4. As the activity takes place, the counselor can track the process and experiences taking place.
5. Once all the prompts have been completed, the school counselors provide time and space for group members to look through their own 'Termination Capsule.' Group members are asked for their reactions.
6. The counselors model interpersonal sharing and self-disclosure through reading aloud the components of their own 'Termination Capsule' that has just been completed. Group members are then invited to share as much of their respective 'Termination Capsules' as they are comfortable.
7. Group members begin to process their experiences of the activity.

Processing Questions/Conclusion:

Potential questions that can be used to process during or following the activity are as follows:

- ✓ How might your experience right now, in this moment, reflect your overall group experience?
- ✓ What do you notice happening inside of you? Around you? Between you?
- ✓ With whom might you share this 'Termination Capsule?' Where will you put it?
- ✓ What else about this group experience would you like to put inside the 'Termination Capsule?'
- ✓ Describe when you might refer back to the contents of the 'Termination Capsule?'
- ✓ Which prompt or response is particularly meaningful to you?
- ✓ What remains unsaid/ unspoken?

Cautions:

This activity can be evocative for some group members, and students often describe a delayed reacting to the activity. Therefore, it can be helpful to process the experience of the activity in a subsequent session. While some group members are quick to share the contents of their 'Termination Capsule,' others do not wish to do so. In either case, the motivations for each can be explored.

Additional Comments:

When appropriate developmentally, group members can be involved in the formation of the question prompts. They can contribute ideas for other group members to respond to as part of the 'Termination Capsules.'

The prompt questions can be adjusted based upon the developmental level of group members, as well as the unique group experiences that have taken place. For example, if there were significant conflicts that occurred within the group, the group members might be asked to specifically reflect upon what was learned through that.

About the Group Worker:

Melissa Luke, Ph.D., LMHC, NCC, is a former School Counselor and currently works as an Assistant Professor and Coordinator of School Counseling in the Counseling and Human Services department at Syracuse University.

Rainbow Web
Submitted by MaryLou Ramsey

Goals:
- ✓ Assist members in dealing with their feelings about termination
- ✓ Help members recall, reflect upon, and give feedback to those who have had the greatest impact upon them during the group
- ✓ Provide both members and leaders with a visually powerful, time efficient means of assessing the interpersonal and collective impact of their group experience
- ✓ Make known and reinforce both the spoken (overt) and unspoken (covert) learnings that can occur within a group

Target Population: All ages

Potential Stage/Session(s): Termination stage

Estimated Time Length: 30-45 minutes, depending on group size. If used as a stimulus for more extended discussions of group termination, add approximately one minute per participant for every additional processing question posed.

Materials: 5-8 carefully rolled balls of different colored yarns

Activity: The Rainbow Web provides a useful, nonverbal way of collectively conceptualizing group termination that may be used alone or along with additional group termination activities. Group members are invited to toss various colored balls of yarn to each other in the co-creation of a web of connections. This activity is particularly useful for groups with limited meeting session time frames and/or very large groups that would benefit from a very engaging yet brief group termination exercise.

Specific Directions for Activity:
In this exercise group members are asked to sit in a circle on the floor and quietly think about their experiences in the group and who has touched them the most. Leaders may enhance the staging of this closure exercise by briefly retracing the group's coming together and subsequent journey and then asking members to consider what they will be taking from this experience and who among them has helped them the most, either by deed or example.

The leaders instruct members to do this exercise in silence and then proceed to distribute each of 5-8 colored balls of yarn to different group members seated on the floor around the circle (this makes it easier to throw and catch the balls of yarn). After a brief period of quiet self-reflection, group members are asked to silently and symbolically share their personal feelings and experiences with those with whom they have felt this connection. This symbolic sharing is expressed by tossing the colored balls of yarn to one another, while retaining hold of a piece of the yarn from each ball received and tossed.

Group members who are handed a ball of yarn are instructed to hold the loose end of the ball of yarn they have been given and then to toss the ball to someone else who they feel has emotionally touched them in some way, verbally or nonverbally, throughout the group experience. When another member receives the ball of yarn s/he is to do the same thing, hold a piece of the yarn and then throw the remaining ball to someone else. This process continues until all the balls of yarn have been unfurled.

Very quickly, a Rainbow Web of yarn begins to take shape within the group circle. At times it can be challenging to catch and hold all of these balls of yarn and yarn ends, but it is also important to note that everyone is drawn into the exercise and often no one wants to let go of their yarn holdings when the exercise is over. Should this be the case, there is another step that can be added to this exercise. Specifically, it is possible to tie each person's yarn bundle together with a small knot, carefully wrap the huge collective Rainbow Web of yarn between large sheets of paper to preserve its shape, and later hang/display the final group yarn representation, along with any identifying year or group name, as an office "group remembrance" decoration.

Group leaders may use the following instructions for this activity:
 ✓ Come together in a circle and quietly and silently think about your experiences in this group (i.e., what have you learned, who has helped you the most whether in deed or by example)
 ✓ Now take the balls of yarn being distributed, hold a piece of the colored yarn so you don't lose its contact and then throw it to someone in the circle whom you feel has touched you the most
 ✓ When the yarn ball comes to you, hold a piece of it and then throw it on to someone else you feel you have connected with throughout this group experience, but please don't comment or talk while doing so, just watch/observe as this web unfolds

Leaders should conclude the yarn toss exercise with a few moments of extended silent reflection on the Rainbow Web of yarn the group members have just created. Following this silent reflection, leaders can offer their own closure observations and/or invite the members to share their experiences. For example, members could be asked to consider what they see/feel/have experienced creating this rainbow tapestry web, what they are taking from this experience, and any other debriefing questions the leaders may want to pose, given the time remaining.

Processing Questions/Conclusion:
 ✓ As you look at this rainbow of colors what feelings, reactions or observations would you like to share with anyone in this group or with the group as a whole?
 ✓ Is there anything else that you would like this tapestry of color to reflect (about what you have learned from your group as a whole or from someone in particular)?
 ✓ How will you weave what you have learned from this group experience into your everyday life and relationships?
 ✓ What are you most likely to miss when you leave this rainbow tapestry experience behind?
 ✓ What is the most important thing that you are taking with you as you release this tapestry and say good-bye to this group?

Cautions:
- ✓ At times the group can want to talk and comment on the evolving web and the leaders will need to remind them to remain quiet.
- ✓ Some members will receive more tosses than others and leaders will need to take this into consideration when processing, but it is highly unlikely that any member will be left out.
- ✓ There are times when flying yarn balls can be a bit overwhelming and even difficult to catch, but the balls themselves are not terribly dangerous, unless someone is allergic to wool.
- ✓ Younger children may need to be reminded to remain in place so as not to add bumping into one another as an additional risk
- ✓ All ages can occasionally lose their grip on a few strands of yarn, but continued tosses will usually compensate for the "drops."
- ✓ Should this exercise be used in consort with a series of additional closure discussion exercises and reflections occurring over multiple weeks' duration, it is recommended that the rainbow tapestry web be one of the last exercises used because its impact tends to diminish with extended debriefing and/or sequel closure exercises.

Additional Comments:

This "Rainbow Web" exercise has been used in a very different, more content specific, capacity during the working stage of a group focusing on HIV/AIDS prevention and education. In the latter, the "Rainbow Web" exercise was used to illustrate the exponential way in which the HIV/AIDS virus can be transmitted and thus the importance of protected sex as a means of prevention.

About the Group Worker:

MaryLou Ramsey, Ed.D., NCC, NCSC, is a Professor and School Counseling Program Coordinator in the Department of Counselor Education at The College of New Jersey.

Feeling Head Group
Submitted by Adam P. Zagelbaum

Goals:
- ✓ Identify personal feelings, recognize that feelings are not always equal to thoughts
- ✓ Make salient connections between how feelings are contained within the head
- ✓ Be able to communicate more directly about feelings and let them out in appropriate manners
- ✓ Understand that one has the power to alter his/her own feelings

Target Population: All ages

Potential Stage/Session(s): Any stage or session

Estimated Time Length: 30 minutes or less

Materials:
- ✓ A round, transparent container which can be glass or plastic
- ✓ Materials that can be drawn or affixed to the container in order to create the image of a human face (such as sketched eyes, or an affixed mouth made of paper)
- ✓ Business-sized or larger-sized cards with feeling words printed on them

Activity: In this activity, group members work as a team to fill and then empty a "feeling head" with feelings. By doing this metaphorical exercise, members become better able to communicate feelings to one another as a result of the ensuing group dynamics. The Feeling Head Group Exercise is an adaptation of the exercise known as The Feeling Head, by Adam Zagelbaum, which appears in *The Therapists' Notebook: Volume II* (Hecker & Sori, 2007).

Specific Directions for Activity:
Gather the group members together and briefly present information related to how feelings can have an impact on our thoughts, views, and behaviors. Mention that some people have difficulty knowing what their feelings are or how to read feelings that show on other people's faces. However, when we know how to do these things, we can become better at addressing feelings and helping other people work through more difficult ones.

The leader may explain as follows:
- ✓ We all have feelings. Sometimes we feel good about ourselves and the way things are, and sometimes we do not. However, sometimes we can feel many different things at the same time, and we may not know how to sort these things out. We know something is probably affecting us, but it may be hard to see how, or to say how to other people.

✓ It seems like all of our feelings are swimming around inside of our head [at that moment, the leader can take out the feeling cards and display the feeling head to the group]. Now, I am going to tell you a story about someone who has some things going on in his life. Pay attention to me as I read the story, and think about some of the things he may be feeling.

At that moment, hold up the "feeling head" container and show it to the group. Also, take the cards which contain the feeling words and place them either on a nearby desk or on the ground in the middle of the group. State to the members that they are going to hear a story about a student and see if they can recognize some of the feelings that may be involved

> *Mike was about to go to his grandmother's house for Thanksgiving. It seemed. different for him this time, though, because this would be the first time that his grandfather would not be there. He passed away from a heart attack about three months ago, and although Mike attended the funeral and recognized the fact that his grandfather was no longer living, it still seemed. odd to him that he was not going to be able to see his grandfather at the dinner table. His mother and father seemed. to know that something different was happening this Thanksgiving as well, but nobody seemed. to be speaking about it.*

> *The drive to his grandmother's house seemed kind of long and quiet, and he wasn't sure what to expect when he finally got there. However, once Mike got to his grandmother's house and saw her waiting for everyone with a big smile on her face, he noticed that things were going to be ok, even though his grandfather would not be physically there. He seemed. to recognize that because people like his grandmother were still around to share memories of his grandfather, he could see that it helps him deal with some of the things that seemed. different about this year's Thanksgiving dinner.*

After a response is given by a group member about a feeling related to the story's main character, the leader asks the member to grab the card that contains the feeling word mentioned, and places it into the "feeling head." The leader asks for other group members to state how the child within the story may be feeling, and place another card with the corresponding word into the "head."

After all responses are completed, the leader holds up the container which displays all of the cards placed within it to the group. As a result of this exercise, members can visually see how their feelings can metaphorically bunch up within their head. The feelings can impact the way they view things, speak about things, and hear things because of the fact that each of these items are displayed on the feeling head.

The leader then asks the group members to come up with some ways of getting these feelings to "come out of their head," such as by telling people how they feel, releasing tears, or listening to other people empathize with their feelings. As these responses are made, the leader removes the cards from the "head" in order to show the group that by communicating to people about their feelings, their "heads" can become clear.

Group can conclude at this point, and it is the leader's decision to assign homework to members related to the labeling or communication of feelings.

Processing Questions/Conclusion:

- ✓ It seems like all of our feelings are swimming around inside of our head. How do you think the story's character (Mike, in this case) is feeling right now?
- ✓ What might happen to Mike if he only keeps his feelings to himself (inside of his head)? What are some things that you/we can do to help Mike clear his head of some of these awkward feelings?
- ✓ How do these things that you/we have come up with relate to what you/we can do for others at school, in this group, and elsewhere?

Credit/References:

Adapted from:

The feeling head. In L. Hecker & K. Sori (Eds.). (2007). *The therapists' notebook: Volume II: More homework, handouts, and activities for use in psychotherapy (pp. xx-xx)*. New York: Haworth Press.

About the Group Worker:

Adam P. Zagelbaum, Ph.D., NCC, is an Assistant Professor in the Counseling Program at Sonoma State University with primary teaching responsibilities in School Counseling.

Building Bridges
Submitted by Rachel Vitale

Goals:
- ✓ Work cooperatively as a team by successfully completing the task of building a bridge without verbal communication

Target Populations: All ages
To participate, students must have the physical ability to stand on one or both feet. In addition, this activity is ideal for larger groups such as classroom guidance groups (10-20 students).

Potential Stage/Session(s): Orientation or transition stage

Estimated Time Length: 20-25 Minutes

Materials:
- ✓ 30-40 vinyl poly spot markers or bases, and four cones (these can usually be borrowed from the physical education department).

Activity:
This engaging, team-building activity uses a scenario involving a desert island and shark infested water to encourage group cohesion and cooperation.

Specific Directions for Activity:
Divide the children into two equal groups and give them these instructions:

- ✓ You are on a desert island and you have to build a bridge to get off of the island. You must work with your team to build a bridge off of the island. (Hand the kids a stack of poly spots or bases with two more of the poly spots then kids on the team.) For example if there are 8 kids on the team, they can have 10 bases/poly spots. Have cones marking the beginning and ending points with the space in between being the "water." Students may have both feet on one poly spot, two feet on two ploy spots, or whatever it is they need to do to not fall off of the bridge as long as it is safe.
- ✓ The water is also infested with sharks so if anyone on the team falls off into the water, the other kids have to rescue her/him and go back to the beginning and start all over.
- ✓ There also happen to be headhunters on the island so the kids have to make sure they pick up the bases/poly spots so that there are none left in the "water" when they get to the other side.
- ✓ When the last person on the team is past the cone marking the finish line then they are all safe. If the last person falls off even at the end everyone has to start over.
- ✓ The final rule is that there is no talking!

Processing Questions/Conclusion:
Following the activity, bring the students into a discussion circle. Examples of processing questions include the following:
- ✓ What was like to not to be able to talk?
- ✓ What was the most difficult part of the task?
- ✓ What was it like for the first person?
- ✓ What was it like for the last person?
- ✓ Do you wish the activity would have gone differently?

If time allows, let students repeat the game with the same rules, except they are allowed to talk. Process the differences between the two experiences.

Cautions:
If one team has the hang of the activity and the other does not use them as an example by saying something like "it looks like team one has the hang of this." The kids on the other team will get it quickly after this. It is critical that the facilitator encourage students to work as a team. This activity works exceptionally well with students who are traditionally the more "difficult students," however it is important to have strong leadership when working with this type of student.

About the Group Worker:
Rachel Vitale has a Master's degree in School Counseling and is pursuing her Ph.D. in Counselor Education at Kent State University in Kent, Ohio.

Frustration Toss

Submitted by Lauren Fugate

Goals:

- ✓ Discuss and process frustrations
- ✓ Relate effectively to others and understand that everyone becomes frustrated
- ✓ Find common ground with people you typically may disagree or conflict with (even teachers or authority figures)

Target population: All ages
Participants should include authority figures and subordinates (students and teachers)

Potential Stage/Session: Transition or working stage

Estimated Time: 1 hour (could be shortened or extended depending on processing and time constraints)

Materials: three sheets of paper per participant and writing utensils; open area with some sort of line/boundary in middle (could use line, masking tape, paper, etc.-- anything to divide the room into two sides.

Introduction:
Explain that everyone deals with frustrations at work/school/home and these vary from teachers to students and supervisors to subordinates. We do not always acknowledge or understand others' perspectives, and in this activity we are going to all process personal work/school related frustrations. This activity will allow us to physically experience others throwing their frustrations on us, which can often happen, and the challenge of taking care of ourselves while not allowing others' frustrations to influence our success.

Activity:
Begin group by asking group "What frustrates you here?" Instruct participants to allow open discussion in identifying frustrations (e.g. people, people's actions, rules, etc.). Following this short discussion, give each participant three sheets of paper and writing instrument, and instruct them to pick three things that frustrate them the most. Once everyone is done, have the group members wad up paper into paper balls.

Divide participants into two teams, one on each side of the dividing line (try to put people who typically disagree or conflict on the same team and ones that get along best on the opposite side). The group leader now divides the paper wads evenly on the floor on both sides of the boundary. The group leader instructs participants not to pick up any paper wads until told to do so. The group will be instructed to have a paper wad fight (not aiming at people) by getting rid of their paper wads, and the team with the fewest on their side of the boundary when time is called will be the winners of this portion of the activity. Set time for approximately 15 minutes, and instruct participants to throw only one paper wad at a time. In order to count, the paper wad must cross the boundary line.

Processing Questions/Conclusion:

- ✓ What is the purpose of this activity?
- ✓ How did it feel throwing your frustrations on others?
- ✓ What insights can be gained from discussing and relating to others frustrations and then physically throwing them on to others when do not have to be held accountable for them?
- ✓ After processing have each participant draw a paper wad and read the frustration on it. Improving or helping others deal with this over the next week will become each person's personal goal.

Cautions:

Make sure authority figures are aware that subordinates are not punished or reprimanded for voicing opinions and issues and that all are allowed to openly voice issues. This is not a time to argue or confront; it is just a time to state and acknowledge issues and concerns.

About the Group Worker:

Lauren Fugate has a master's degree in Mental Health Counseling and is involved with group and individual counseling through Helen Ross McNabb Center in Knoxville, TN with at-risk youth enrolled in the ABC IV classroom.

People I Really, Deeply Admire

Submitted by Brian Mistler

Goals:
- ✓ Develop a clearer sense of personal values
- ✓ Become aware of social and media influences
- ✓ Develop group support and cohesion

Target Population: All ages

Potential Stage/Session(s): Any stage or session

Estimated Time Length: 20-30 minutes, 2-3 minutes per participant minimum. Flexible time length depending on processing.

Materials: Paper and pencil (optional)

Activity: This activity allows group members to clarify their personal values by identifying, recording and sharing the traits in other people they admire. In the context of the group, social and media influences may be explored and processed.

Specific Directions for Activity:
Introduction should emphasize picking people we "really, deeply admire." This helps set the stage for a more value focused choice and discussion. Individuals usually choose people different than those in the popular media or, at minimum, qualities different from those generally highlighted as 'in fashion'.

Group members are asked to think of (or write down) the names of 2-3 people they "really, deeply, admire." Next, group members are asked to identify (and if paper is available make a written list of) the traits in these people which they find most admirable. As a final step, if the leader feels it is appropriate, group members may be invited to share with the group as a whole or in smaller triads.

After group members share their selections, process questions can be used to guide the conversation in a number of directions depending on the nature of the group. After processing, activity could also lead into various projects (e.g., making ideal self portraits of who individuals would like to become, writing letters to people they admire sharing their feelings, writing letters or sharing words of admiration with one another in the group, cutting out images from popular magazines which do/do not represent their "deep values" and forming a collage.

Processing Questions/Conclusion:
  ✓ How did you choose those people? What qualities stand out most?
  ✓ How do your choices compare to others in the group? Are you surprised that they're similar or different in any way?
  ✓ How do the values of the people you admire reflect who <u>you</u> are? How are those values reflected in your life? If people listened to the things you say and saw the things you do, what would they think your deep values were?
  ✓ Do your parents really, deeply admire any of the same people you do? Have you ever asked them who they really, deeply admire?
  ✓ Do you get messages from parents or television that the people you really, deeply admire you shouldn't? Who do your parents, friends, or television tell you to think is cool?
  ✓ What do you do <u>already</u> that other people might really, deeply admire about you? What do you admire about yourself? What do you wish more people understood about you?
  ✓ What do you do that stops people from getting to know or admiring you?
  ✓ Do these people you admire know how you feel? How do you think they might feel if you told them? If you haven't told them, what stops you?
  ✓ Do these people you admire have flaws? Does that prevent you from admiring them? (If individuals pick historical icons like Mahatma Ghandi or the Rev. Dr. M. L. King it's especially important to talk about their struggles as real people. If they choose parents or grandparents it's also important to talk about specific qualities that they like and things they saw them do that let them know about these qualities).
  ✓ How do you think the people you really, deeply admire deal with their problems and shortcomings? What's it like to be human and imperfect? How can you be more accepting of yourself, even with your own flaws?

Cautions:
Not recommended for groups with extremely low verbal ability.

About the Group Worker:
Brian Mistler has a master's degree in Conflict Resolution from The University of Bradford, U.K., and is finishing a Ph.D. in Counseling Psychology at the University of Florida.

Fantasy Shopping
Submitted by MaryLou Ramsey

Goals:
- ✓ Help members test the group atmosphere and get acquainted
- ✓ Promote initial, low-risk personal sharing and expression of feelings and thoughts
- ✓ Build trust and group cohesion

Session Goals with the Progressive Assessment Option: To a) assess members' personal development over the course of the group, b) assist members in sharing what they are feeling and thinking as the group evolves, and c) assess the evolution of the group as a collective.

Target Population: All ages

Potential Stage/Session(s): Any stage or session

Estimated Time Length: One minute per person with a minimum of 15-20 minutes for processing, depending on the number of questions posed.

Materials:
No materials are required

Activity:
This engaging activity uses various shopping departments or areas as a way to share personal characteristics, observations and/or group process and development over time. The group may be adapted in a variety of ways to accommodate a range of group needs.

Specific Directions for Activity:
Ask students to imagine themselves in a favorite multi-service store or shopping area that the leaders identify as appropriate to their experience, socioeconomic status, cultural background, age, and potential interests (i.e., Wal-Mart's or Toys R Us). Tell them to think about what department/area they identify with the most and what item in that department/area would best represent them at this moment in time.

Allow enough time for students to imagine this scenario and then ask them to share and explain their choice. For elementary school children, the leaders could begin this exercise by asking them to imagine that they are walking through several different areas of the store, and then rephrase their fantasy question in more concrete terms, such as "If you could be anything in this store right now, what would you be and why?"

When this activity is used in the initial stage/session of a group, processing questions and/or observations should be held to a minimum until all have shared. At the conclusion of the full group sharing, the leader(s) can offer their own observations of common themes and feelings, unique and/or different disclosures and invite students to elaborate, as time permits, before moving on to discuss other introductory issues such as member expectations, group time and duration, and confidentiality.

If the leader(s) wish to use this activity as an ongoing evaluation exercise to assess members' personal development over the course of the group, then they can repeat this exercise at various points throughout the group (i.e., transition, working, and termination stages). During these subsequent uses, students may be asked to consider such things as: changes over time, similarities and differences, surprises, themes, patterns, and evidence of growth in themselves and in the group as a whole.

Processing Questions/Conclusion:
- ✓ What were your thoughts as you made this selection?
- ✓ How are you feeling about this selection at this point in time?
- ✓ Is this selection similar or different from your previous one? Can you explain?
- ✓ How is this item/selection like you right now?
- ✓ What are some of the similarities and/or differences you see in your selection, yourself and/or someone else?
- ✓ Are there any surprises you're experiencing that you want to share with the group?

Processing Questions with the Progressive Assessment Option:
- ✓ What themes and/or patterns do you see in your responses over the course of this group?
- ✓ Do you think someone close to you would purchase this item? Who and why or why not?
- ✓ What department/area is least like you and what item in that department/area would least represent you at this moment in time? Can you elaborate?
- ✓ Consider if both areas (your preferred area and your least preferred) are reflections of you are as a person, what does this tell you about yourself? How do you feel about these contrasting aspects?
- ✓ What do your selections indicate about how you have changed?
- ✓ What do others' selections indicate about how they as individuals have, or the group as a whole has, changed?
- ✓ What have you learned about yourself as a result of this progressive group activity and group experience?

Cautions:
- ✓ Some members may have difficulty fantasizing
- ✓ Selection of "appropriate" shopping area/store must be done with careful attention to socioeconomic, cultural, age and other related variables
- ✓ Selections and rationale for same need to be time-monitored to afford everyone a chance to share within the same group session
- ✓ Young children are likely to favor toys they want and require additional prompting to link their selections to themselves
- ✓ As with all group exercises, leaders need to be prepared for selections that disclose personal and/or family hardships that require auxiliary support and intervention

About the Group Worker:
MaryLou Ramsey, Ed.D., NCC, NCSC, is a Professor and School Counseling Program Coordinator in the Department of Counselor Education at The College of New Jersey.

Out With the Trash!
Submitted by Jeri L. Crowell

Goals:
- ✓ Facilitate group members' affective release
- ✓ Improve negative focus on factors within the group functioning
- ✓ Help lively youngsters calm down and regain a more positive group focus

Target population: All ages

Potential Stage/Session(s): Any stage or session

Estimated Time Length: 25-30 minutes with processing

Materials: A small to medium size trash can

Activity: Have all members sit in a tight circle around the garbage can. Instruct the students to "talk to the garbage can" all at once about what is most on their minds, i.e., thoughts that distract them from fully participating in the group at that time, negative thoughts and words about other group members, and/or any excess energy that prohibits them from sitting still long enough to participate beneficially in the group. The leader calls "STOP" at some point and insists on quiet. Process the activity as described.

Specific Directions for Activity:
The group leader must first gather the attention of all group members and get them to physically move the garbage can to a central position while all members place themselves tightly around it. Group members will be instructed to imagine that they will be placing their least helpful thoughts and feelings in the garbage can by actually talking to it.

Processing Questions/Conclusion:
- ✓ What did it feel like to talk to the garbage can?
- ✓ Once you released all of that talk or energy, what do you think is in its place now?
- ✓ What was most difficult about keeping up your own conversation with the garbage can?
- ✓ What did you like best about this activity?
- ✓ What did you like least about this activity?
- ✓ What is another way that you can release troublesome thoughts or excess energy?

Cautions:
It is possible for the activity to become loud and students can become very excited. This is particularly true of younger students. When introducing the activity, be sure to emphasize that there might be limitations to the noise level or volume.

Additional Comments:
This activity is interesting when students need an appropriate way to vent feelings/attitudes or to express negative influences in their lives. What the group leader does to follow up can be very therapeutic or this activity can just be fun.

Credit/References:
Conyne, R., Crowell, J., & Newmeyer, M. (2008). *Group techniques: How to use them more purposefully.* Upper Saddle River, NJ: Pearson Prentice Hall.

About the Group Worker:
Jeri L. Crowell, Ed.D., NCC, LPC, is an Assistant Professor in Counselor Education at Fort Valley State University in Fort Valley, Georgia.

208

Groups Organized by Appropriate Stage

Orientation Stage

Transition Stage

Working Stage

Termination Stage

Any Stage

212

Author Index

About the Editors

Louisa L. Foss is an Assistant Professor in the Counseling and School Psychology program at Southern Connecticut State University in New Haven, Connecticut. Prior to her appointment at Southern, she taught at Walsh University in North Canton, Ohio. Dr. Foss received her Bachelor's degree from The Ohio State University and attended Kent State University for her Master's degree in Community Counseling and Ph.D. in Counselor Education and Supervision. As a Licensed Professional Clinical Counselor (Ohio) and National Certified Counselor (NCC), Dr. Foss has practiced in agency, school, and correctional settings. She significantly contributed to the development of the group counseling program at Child Guidance Centers in Akron, Ohio and served as a counselor and clinical supervisor at a facility for juvenile delinquents in Canton, Ohio. In addition, Dr. Foss has provided school-based mental health services to elementary, middle, and secondary schools in northeast Ohio.

Dr. Foss' areas of interest include group work with adolescents, counseling ethics, and counselor professional development. She has served as President of the Ohio ASGW, President of the Ohio ASERVIC, and as Co-Chair of the Ethics Committee for the Ohio Counseling Association. Dr. Foss has several publications, including articles in the *Journal for Specialists in Group Work* and *Counseling and Values*. She has had numerous presentations at the national level on topics such as partner violence, juvenile delinquency, counseling student development, and group work with children and adolescents.

Judy Green is an Associate Professor in the Counseling and Human Development Program at Walsh University in North Canton, Ohio where she teaches both mental health and school counseling courses and serves as the Coordinator of the School Counseling Program.

Dr. Green received her Bachelor's degree from Thiel College in Greenville, Pennsylvania, earned two Master's degrees from Kent State University, one in early Childhood Education and one in School Counseling. She also earned her Ph.D. in Counselor Education and Supervision from Kent State University. Dr. Green is a Licensed Clinical Counselor with supervisory status (Ohio) and a permanently certified School Counselor (Ohio). She holds both the National Certified Counselor (NCC) and National Certified School Counselor (NCSC) credentials.

Dr. Green brings significant experience to her teaching both as a school counselor and as a clinical counselor. She worked 30 years as a public school teacher and school counselor before joining the Walsh staff. Since 1995, she has worked as a Counselor Educator and mental health practitioner in private practice. Her research and professional interests include grief and trauma counseling, working as a volunteer mental health counselor for the local Red Cross, women's issues, child and adolescent counseling, as well as training and supervising newly licensed counselors. She is currently President-Elect of the

Ohio ASGW and has served on numerous state and local counseling committees. Dr. Green has several publications on topics in school counseling. She has presented locally, nationally and internationally on topics such as grief reactions among children, maladaptive grief reactions to chronic loss and sorrow, depression among the elderly, and issue surrounding deployment and re-entry among military families.

Kelly Wolfe-Stiltner is a licensed School Counselor at an elementary school in Fort Wayne, Indiana. Ms. Wolfe-Stiltner received her Bachelor's degree in secondary education from Ball State University and Master's degree in school counseling from Indiana University Purdue University Fort Wayne. Ms. Wolfe-Stiltner has five years of teaching experience at a residential treatment facility. She also has taught a professional orientation and ethics class to school counselors.

Ms. Wolfe-Stiltner's areas of interest include group work, grief work, ethical and legal issues in school counseling and the role of the school counselor. She has served as a Media Committee Co-Chair and committee member for ASGW.

Janice DeLucia-Waack is an Associate Professor and Program Director of the School Counseling program in the Department of Counseling, School, and Educational Psychology at the University at Buffalo, SUNY. She is the former editor of the *Journal for Specialists in Group Work*, and is a Fellow in the Association for Specialists in Group Work and American Psychological Association Division 49: Group Psychology and Group Psychotherapy. She is author of three books: *Leading Psychoeducational Groups for Children and Adolescents, Multicultural Counseling and Training: Implications and Challenges for Practice* and *Using Music in Children of Divorce Groups: A Session-By-Session Manual for Counselors;* and co-author of another three books: *Group Work Experts Share Their Favorite Activities: A Guide to Choosing, Planning, Conducting, and Processing* (with Karen Bridbord, Jennifer Kleiner, and Amy Nitza) and *The Practice of Multicultural Group Work: Visions and Perspectives from the Field* (with Jeremiah Donigian), and *Handbook of Group Counseling and Psychotherapy* (with Debbie Gerrity, Cynthia Kalodner, and Maria Riva). Dr. DeLucia-Waack is a former Secretary of APA Division 49 and current President of the Association for Specialists in Group Work.

She received a bachelor's degree in Psychology from Eisenhower College, a Master's degree in Family Studies from the University of Maryland, and a Ph.D. in Counseling Psychology from the Pennsylvania State University. Her counseling and research interests include: the process and therapeutic factors related to psychoeducational and counseling groups, school counseling and support services in the schools, eating disorders and body image, children of divorce, supervision, and multicultural issues.

The Association for Specialists in Group Work (ASGW)

What is ASGW?

The Association for Specialists in Group Work was founded in 1973.

The purposes of ASGW are to:
• Establish standards for professional and ethical group practice.
• Support research and the dissemination of knowledge related to group work.
• Provide leadership and training in group specialties.

In addition, ASGW seeks to extend counseling, consulting, and organizational development through group process, to build community through group work, to provide a forum for examining innovative and developing concepts in group work, to foster diversity and dignity in our groups, and to be a model of effective group practice.

Who Joins ASGW?

Members include counselors and other professionals who are interested in and specialize in group work, and who value the creation of community and the provision of group service to members, their clients, and the profession of counseling. Membership is for persons who use group leadership as a process to facilitate the growth and development of people. Applications include mental health agencies, schools, community organizations, colleges and hospitals. To learn more about ASGW, go to www.asgw.org.

Benefits of Joining ASGW

• *Journal for Specialists in Group Work*, a quarterly journal that publishes research and practical and innovative articles of relevance to group practitioners.
• The *Group Worker*, a newsletter published three times annually, providing regional and national news related to group work, legislative updates, and special articles of interest to group practitioners.
• Participation at member rates for ASGW group training events conducted in regional areas across the country. ASGW workshop coordinators work with local sponsors to offer a variety of group training workshops that provide attractive opportunities for continued professional development.
• Local support through state and regional organizations for specialists in group work.

Types of Membership

ASGW membership categories include Professional, Regular, New Professional, Student, and Retired. ACA membership is not required for membership in ASGW.

Professional: Professional members hold a graduate degree in counseling or a closely related field and are engaged in the teaching, practice or research of group work. Professional members have all rights and benefits of membership in ASGW.
Regular: Regular members are members who have an interest in group work, including related professional groups such as social work, psychology, and counselors from countries other than the United States. Regular members have all rights and benefits of membership in ASGW, except holding elective office.
New Professional: A New Professional is someone who has graduated with a masters or a doctorate within the past 12 months. Status is good for one year.
Student: Student members are persons who are actively enrolled in a graduate program and studying group work. Student members have all rights and benefits of membership in ASGW, except holding elective office.
Retired: Members who are retired from the counseling profession and have been active ACA and ASGW member for the past 5 consecutive years.

Division Processing Fee

To join ASGW without joining ACA, a processing fee of $10 will apply.

ASGW/ACA Membership Dues
(valid thru 6/30/2008)

ASGW subscribes to and operates under the auspices of the ACA (American Counseling Association) Code of Ethics. By becoming an ASGW member, you are agreeing to be subject to the rules, regulations, and enforcement of the terms of the ACA Code of Ethics, which include appropriate sanctions up to suspension or expulsion from ACA and public notice about any such action. The ACA Code of Ethics of available at www.counseling.org or www.asgw.org

Choose one	ASGW		ACA		Total
Professional	$40.00	+	$151.00	=	$191.00
Regular	$40.00	+	$151.00	=	$191.00
New Professional **	$27.00	+	$85.00	=	$112.00
Student*	$27.00	+	$85.00	=	$112.00
Retired	$27.00	+	$85.00	=	$112.00
Joining ASGW only	ASGW		Processing Fee		Total
Professional	$40.00	+	$10.00	=	$50.00
Regular	$40.00	+	$10.00	=	$50.00
New Professional **	$27.00	+	$10.00	=	$37.00
Student*	$27.00	+	$10.00	=	$37.00
Retired	$27.00	+	$10.00	=	$37.00
Adding ASGW to ACA Membership **(For current ACA members only)** If adding ASGW to a current ACA membership, call Member Services at 800-347-6647 x 222 for prorated dues amount to coordinate with your ACA renewal date.					
Professional ASGW	$40.00		New Professional ASGW	=	$27.00
Student ASGW	$27.00		Retired ASGW	=	$27.00

Join on the Web!
http://www.counseling.org/Counselors/MemberJoin.aspx

Check it Out!

Group Work Experts Share Their Favorite Activities: A Guide to Choosing, Planning, Conducting, and Processing
(Revised Edition)

Revised Edition

GROUP WORK EXPERTS SHARE THEIR FAVORITE ACTIVITIES: A GUIDE TO CHOOSING, PLANNING, CONDUCTING, AND PROCESSING

Revised Edition

Edited by:
DeLucia-Waack
H. Bridbord
Sue Kleiner
Nitza

ISBN 1-55620-265-2

This book presents over 50 group activities in a ready-to-use format with tips for implementation. The activities cover a full range of types and stages of groups. Introductory chapters offer a guide to successful selection, implementation, and processing of structured activities. This book is a must-have practitioner resource as well as an excellent supplemental text.

M & M Game
Paper Bag Skits
Fiddler on the Roof
Feedback as Poetry

To order contact: ACA Order Services
1-800-422-2648 ext. 222 www.counseling.org
5999 Stevenson Avenue, Alexandria, VA 22304

222